Religion and Social Work Practice
in Contemporary American Society

Religion and Social Work Practice in Contemporary American Society

Frank M. Loewenberg

Columbia University Press
New York   1988

Library of Congress Cataloging-in-Publication Data

Loewenberg, Frank M.
  Religion and social work practice in contemporary American society
Frank M. Loewenberg.
    p.   cm.
  Bibliography: p.
  Includes indexes.
  ISBN 0-231-06452-7
  1. Social service—Religious aspects.   2. Social workers—United
States—Religious life.   I. Title.
HV530.L6 1988
361.3'2—dc19

Columbia University Press
New York   Guildford, Surrey
Copyright © 1988 Columbia University Press
Printed in the United States of America

Hardback editions of Columbia University Press books are Smyth-
sewn and are printed on permanent and durable acid-free paper.

To the memory of my father
Ernst L. Loewenberg
1896–1987

Contents

Introductory
Comments

Many are convinced that there is no room for religion in modern scientific social work. But how can they be so sure of this view when most Americans say that they believe in God and when seven out of every ten adults say that they are members of a church or a synagogue? Given these circumstances, it may be important to reexamine the place of religion in social work practice.

Whatever their personal convictions and beliefs, social workers should not close their eyes to the possible impact of religion on social work practice, especially when many of their clients indicate that religion is very important for them. Yet many social workers are uncomfortable when religious questions come up in their practice. Such a response by practitioners may be problematic, especially if we take seriously Victor Frankl's proposition that

Man lives in three dimensions: the somatic, the mental, and the spiritual. The spiritual dimension cannot be ignored, for it is what makes us human. . . . The proper diagnosis can be made only by someone who can see the spiritual side of man. (1968:ix)

For many, if not most Americans, the "spiritual dimension" means religion. It is this that led one prominent social work educator to observe that an "understanding [of] religion is essential for effective practice" (Pins 1960:56). This is one of the factors that led to the writing of this volume.

Another consideration is that the general public, increasingly a conservative public, identifies social workers as radicals, libertarians, and irreligious. Yet a growing number of social workers do not fit this characterization. There are social workers who regularly vote for conservative candidates. Other social workers are church members. Some belong to liberal churches, others to fundamentalist churches. There are Muslim social workers who pray five times a day and Jewish social workers who worship in a synagogue three times a day. The fact that all social workers are not of the same ideological or religious mold raises some important questions. One crucial question is whether the values that a social worker holds make a difference in the way she or he approaches clients. Or are the professional values of the social work profession so firmly internalized that they neutralize or override individual values?

When it comes to religion, there seem to be two types of social workers. One group of practitioners bases its practice on secular, humanist principles which are rooted in the positivist scientific tradition. Formal religion is not relevant for the practice of these social workers. Then there is another group whose practice is rooted in religious beliefs and values. There seems to be so little contact between the members of these two groups that one writer wondered if there were two types of social work: a godly social work and a godless social work (Marty 1980:465). One need not agree completely with this dichotomous description of social work to realize that there exists among social workers a vast amount of misunderstanding, mistrust, and perhaps even alienation concerning religion and its place in professional practice.

In this monograph I intend to explore various issues relevant to the interface of social work and religion. My aim is not to propagandize or to convince anyone to accept or reject this or that doctrine or belief. I will try to avoid closures. Instead I want to indicate points of departure for further study and for additional thought. I want to open windows in order to help students and practitioners to think about these questions so that they can better serve all of their clients, both those with a religious commitment and those for whom religion is of no apparant relevance. I propose to raise issues and topics that have been ignored too often in the professional discourse, and to facilitate an exchange of views between social workers from various backgrounds so that they will know better each other's positions.

In the first part of this book I will develop the background against which I will later examine social work practice problems. Chap-

ter 1 examines the views of social workers about religion and of religionists about social work. The place of religion in contemporary
American society is examined in chapter 2. Values and ideology in
professional practice, especially in social work practice, are the major
subject of chapter 3. In this chapter I will also develop the differences
between religious and secular values and explore the impact of these
on social work practice.

Part 2 will examine various practice issues and dilemmas encountered by social workers. In chapter 4, I note that social workers
who hold religious values, as well as those who do not, may face
practice problems that involve religious issues, though the specific
problems that they may face will not always be the same. I will discuss
the advantages and disadvantages of matching client values with practitioner values, as well as the issue of value judgments, value neutrality,
and value imposition—issues that every social worker encounters
frequently.

Chapter 5 deals with practice issues faced by social workers
when working with religious and/or secular clients. Social workers'
need for sensitivity and empathy, even when it comes to clients who
are quite different from them, is stressed. Practice problems encountered when working with religiously oriented clients may arise from
their beliefs, rituals, or observances. These issues, as well as the use
of prayer in the professional context, are discussed. A special section
examines the relationship between religiosity and psychopathology.

Next I examine the practice implications of such phenomena
as sin and guilt. Special attention is given to the practice skill of
dereflection. Problems arising out of practice with secular clients are
also discussed in this chapter. The discussion concerning the cooperation dilemma will be of particular interest to religiously oriented
social workers.

Chapter 6 is devoted to an exploration of the role of religious
organizations, such as churches and sectarian agencies. The particular
problems arising out of the referral of clients to clergy persons also are
investigated here.

In Part 3, the epilogue, I propose next steps that the social work
profession generally and social work research and education in particular must undertake in order to pierce the wall that seems to stand
between religion and social work.

Titmuss, in the preface to one of his last books, wrote that he had "incurred many social debts . . . gifts solicited and unsolicited, in the form of advice and criticism." I have also been the recipient of many such gifts as I wrote and rewrote this book. It is therefore not prudent to single out the contributions of some and not of others. Nevertheless, I find myself in particular debt to three colleagues, Drs. Naomi Baum, Haya Izhaki, and David Portowitz, who collaborated in a study that whetted my interest in the many questions explored in this book. The thoughtful critique of an anonymous reviewer kept me from making a number of mistakes and resulted, I trust, in a more readable and more useful book. Finally, I would like to thank my wife and helpmate, Chaya, for her many questions and suggestions on various drafts of this book. Needless to say, the responsibility for the interpretations of the data and for any errors is entirely mine.

One final point. The reader may ask whether I "believe." My response to this question is that I do believe and that I do practice my beliefs. However, this book is not about my beliefs or about my theology. It is about social work practice and religion in contemporary American society.

Religion and Social Work Practice
in Contemporary American Society

Part I

Social Work and Religion

Chapter One

Social Work Practice
in a Secular Society

Problems have replaced *mysteries* in the contemporary world (White-head 1948). What is the difference between these two concepts? Mysteries are beyond human knowledge and understanding, while problems can be solved through the application of human intelligence and technology. Many people believe that in a society like ours, one that is based on science and technology, there is no longer any need to refer perplexing questions to the supernatural. Rational principles are all that is needed to solve any problem that may arise.

In this chapter I will discuss the role of the social work profession in such a rational and secular society. I will explore how different social workers view religion and how, in turn, religious people view social work. I will also try to account for the gap or disjunction that has evolved between religious organizations and the social work profession. Finally, I will take note of the place of religious social workers and will try to identify some of the problems they may face.

Social work developed as a secular profession in the modern world. Many social workers, regardless of their personal religious affiliations, do not think that their religion has any particular relevance for everyday professional practice. Just as they are committed to the principle of the separation of church and state in government, so have they accepted the principle of separating the sacred and the profane in their own lives. Some may at times seek answers or reassurances from religious sources, but even for them religion often has become a private, part-time institution which has relatively little bearing on their professional lives (Wilson 1982).

The relationship between the sacred and the profane aspects of life once was a key question for almost everyone. But this question is often no longer of interest or concern. Some social workers say that the "sacred" has faded away altogether or that it has lost relevance for them. There are those who completely reject any of the sacred aspects of life, especially when these seem to interfere with professional requirements. For example, some social workers have urged the repeal of laws that forbid cross-religious adoptions because they believe that these make it impossible to promote the best interests of adoptive children and because they are convinced that religious considerations are rarely relevant to adoption decisions (Gollub 1974).

But other social workers insist that religious values do influence professional social work practice, even the practice of some of those who emphatically deny any connection with religion. They argue that a person need not be consciously aware of any religious influence in order to be affected by it. The mere repudiation of religion by a person does not mean that religion ceases to play a role in that person's life.

Social Workers View Religion

Religion has been defined as "a system of beliefs and practices by means of which a group of people struggle with the ultimate problems of human life" (Yinger 1957:9). But this dry definition fails to convey what religion really means to believers. It also fails to deal adequately with the various functions that religious institutions fulfill in society. The functions and dysfunctions of religion in contemporary society will be discussed in chapter 2. Here, I will explore the more subjective responses of different social workers to religion in general and to religious institutions in particular.

Social workers, as a group, have been described as radical, libertarian, irreligious, even antireligious (Siporin 1984, 1985b). This description may be true for some, perhaps for many, but certainly not for all social workers. At least three general attitudes can be identified that different social workers have held with respect to religion and its impact on practice:

1. Most social workers ignore religion as if it were not relevant to the concerns of the profession. This group includes many who are practicing Christians, Muslims, or Jews in their personal lives.

2. Other social workers, a much smaller number, attack religion (usually implicitly, but sometimes explicitly) as harmful to the client and as opposed to the goals and values of the profession. Generally, those found in this category are not active in any religious group, but some may be affiliated with a liberal or humanistic religious group.

3. Still other social workers, less prominent in the literature and possibly fewer in number, attribute to religion a central role in both their personal and professional lives.

A Fragmented Literature

The social work literature generally has ignored or dismissed the impact of religion on practice. One author who expressed concern about this noted that "the professional literature addressed to religion and social work has been slow to develop and has been for the most part a fragmented literature" (Judah 1985:26). Aside from articles written by believers who are bothered by this void, I have found only a few instances of serious professional concern with this subject (e.g., Biestek 1953; Spencer 1956). Even authors who mention religion often do so as an aside or as an afterthought; for example, Towle's classic *Common Human Needs* is a book of 174 pages, but only sixteen lines are devoted to the "spiritual needs" of the individual (1965:11).

In recent years there has been some change in the professional climate. The publication of a number of articles and the growing number of presentations on religious themes at national conferences is one indication of increasing interest in this question. However, the avoidance syndrome is still so strong that many of these articles and speeches deal with "moral questions and ethical issues" because their authors feel that a direct reference to religion would not receive a sympathetic hearing from many of their colleagues (e.g., Goldstein 1986; Siporin 1985a; Siporin and Glasser 1987).

Various reasons have been advanced for the fact that the social work literature "genially and serenely ignores religion" (Marty 1980:465). These include:

1. The scientific method and a rational approach to the world is believed to be essential for a practice field that wants to be recognized as a profession. Since religion is viewed as the antithesis to science, it is best ignored.

2. Religious values are believed to be in conflict with basic social work values such as client self-determination and worker nonjudgmentalism.

3. Religion emphasizes the spiritual and the otherworldly. This emphasis leads to a neglect of basic human and social needs, the very areas that are of major concern to social workers.

4. Religion, by supporting the status quo, has tended to support the capitalist system and in this way perpetuates all of the social injustices that that system has created.

5. Religious teachings tend to inculcate prejudice, promote conflict, and generate pathology among believers.

Some are even more critical and maintain that religion is an expression of neurotic helplessness and dependence which inevitably results in warped minds and crippling experiences. They believe that religious worship is "an atavism left over from primitive magic and animism" and that no effort should be spared to help people abandon such a delibitating activity (Zilboorg 1962:227). The prevalence of this type of thinking was confirmed for me recently in one of my seminars for doctoral students. An experienced social worker told me that "alcohol, religion, and drugs" were pathological responses used by people who cannot cope adequately with life's problems. When I asked him which of the three was the most damaging, he replied that he thought all three were equally damaging!

Among those who have taken note of the damaging effects of religion on human behavior, social policy decisions, and other aspects of daily life are not only aggressive and radical atheists, but even some liberal theologians who have warned against the negative aspects of traditional religion. Though they affirm that religion may be a positive force, they note that it also contains damaging elements. They are particularly concerned about the rigid ritualism and inflexible doctrines that they say characterize many fundamentalist religious groups.

Linking Social Work and Religion

On the other hand, there are social workers who have tried to link religion and social work. Best known among these are Biestek, Bowers, Keith-Lucas, Siporin, and Spencer. But many other practitioners have followed a secular, humanist approach to practice and have rejected any such linkage attempts. Some of them believe that the desire to link religion and social work reflects unresolved personal needs. They are convinced that such attempts are not professional and will harm the scientific status of the profession. Still other social workers suggest that religion and social work are essentially two incompatible systems; they conclude, therefore, that it makes little sense to attempt to unite or integrate them. These social workers have no difficulty in separating the two systems since they believe that each deals with a different world of interest. Among this last group one can even find some who attend church on Sundays and who take an active role in church committees, but who do not let religious values influence their professional practice patterns.

　　Many social workers do not reject religion, but have raised doubts about its effectiveness in problem solving. They indicate that religion is not a therapeutic method and that religious belief solves neither concrete nor emotional problems. Some cite Freud's observation that "it is doubtful whether men were in general happier at a time when religious doctrines held unlimited sway than they are now" (1957:67). Others suggest that social workers who emphasize religion and religous questions in their practice not only fail to ease or solve a client's difficult personal problems, but may actually cause additional complications.

Pluralistic Religion

It is important to emphasize that one must be cautious in generalizing about religion. Different denominations and faith communities are quite different from one another. They make different demands on their followers and have different effects on society. Though all are identified as religious groups, a mainline Protestant group has a different impact on the everyday life of its members than does a Pentacostal one, and these, in turn, are quite different from the more esoteric cults that are based on Eastern cultures. Many social workers, like most other people, react to religion in terms of the specific religion they know best; while they first reject or accept a specific religion, not religion in general, they subsequently generalize from their own specific experience to religion in general. This is an undesirable generalization which a professional practitioner should avoid because it is often inaccurate. A particular religious experience may have been damaging or rewarding, satisfying or destructive; but this need not mean that all other religious experiences will have the identical impact.

The doctrinal differences among different religious faiths, even between different denominations within the same faith, have confused many people. One theologian noted that "Christianity in its twenty centuries and many lands is a Protean thing and nowhere does it seem more diverse and multifarious than in America" (Niebuhr 1937:2). Contradictions, reversals, and polarizations are all too common. These make it impossible to "verify" what is really "good," let alone what is "true." It is not possible to establish what "religion" thinks on any issue because for every religious authority who says yes to a given position, there is another who says no. Even American evangelicals are not a monolithic group, though they do reflect a high degree of consensus. Quebedeaux (1974) identified five types of evangelicals, ranging from closed fundamentalists on the right to radical evangelicals on the left. For example, some evangelicals make a strong case for an affirmative stance toward homosexuals (Scanoni and Mollenkott 1978), a view that is entirely rejected by most other evangelical Christians.

Differences in religious doctrines and religious practices are not necessarily the consequences of attempts to adjust to modernism and pluralism. Many more bitter, even bloody schisms occurred in all of the major religions in antiquity and in the Middle Ages than in modern times. The Catholic church, often cited as an example of a centralized, monolithic church, is no exception. Throughout history it contained within its fold many different philosophies and schools of thought. Thus, in the sixteenth century the Spanish Mendicants viewed the problem of the poor radically different than did the Italian Jesuits, even though both were religious orders in the same Roman Catholic Church (Pullan 1971).

Social Problems and the Church

It has been said that religion focuses on spiritual matters and is indifferent to the burning social problems that face contemporary society. This is one of the reasons that led many to leave the Church. For example, many people in nineteenth-century England were said to have been appalled by the failure of devout Christians to protest society's callous attitude toward unmarried mothers. When the members of the English parliament determined in the Poor Law of 1834 that the woman alone was responsible for a child born out of wedlock, no major religious institution or religious leader spoke out against this heartless provision of the law (Hall and Howes 1965). No doubt there were church groups, then as now, that did not approve this stance, but their views were not heard in the public forums. Instead, these churches concentrated their efforts on providing services. Even though some of the pioneer services for unmarried mothers were established and operated by religious groups, many people concluded that religion was not concerned with the tragic consequences of industrialism and urbanism.

Similar developments occurred in America. Though religious groups were among the first to provide welfare services, many people began to question the churches' commitment to the ideals of social justice. Some churches and some religious leaders realized relatively early that the poor and the disadvantaged needed much more than the spiritual aid that many churches did provide early in the nineteenth century. Thus, the evangelical New York City Tract Society took an active part in establishing the New York Association for Improving the Condition of the Poor (AICP), one of the pioneer welfare organizations in North America. AICP had by the 1840s already established a comprehensive relief system with district visitors (Smith 1957). Chicago's churches, both Protestant and Catholic, were in the forefront of those that provided welfare services in that frontier city. When during the

1849 cholera epidemic Chicago's poorhouse was so badly overcrowded that orphan children were turned away, the city's Protestant churches united to sponsor the first orphan asylum in Chicago. Popular preachers, like the revivalist Charles Grandison Finney, demanded that religious conversion be followed by social action, thus insuring a steady flow of volunteers to staff the many charities and welfare services (McCarthy 1982:8, 59; Walch 1978).

In the years after the Civil War, the "institutional church" reflected the social concerns of many Protestant churches. City rescue missions, often nondenominational, were established to offer food, shelter, and rehabilitation to "derelicts." The Social Gospel was a serious attempt to develop a Christian theological basis for social concern and social reform (Hammond and Johnson 1970:142–46). Comparable developments occurred somewhat later among Catholics and Jews. In time, these services evolved into the extensive structure of sectarian agencies which currently fill a significant role in every American city. But despite these practical demonstrations of social concern, the impression remained that religious institutions lacked understanding and sympathy for the poor and downtrodden. Some believed that the churches' social concerns were directed primarily toward conversion activities. The large masses of immigrants from Catholic countries were wary about the proselytizing of Protestant groups, no matter how well-meaning their activities. The unorganized factory workers often felt that the church was yet another organization that worked at the behest of their employer. Whether or not these perceptions were accurate is less important than the fact that they persuaded many to abandon the church. Some of these turned instead to the emerging social work profession, which they thought did express these concerns in a very practical way.

The idea for the now discredited division of the poor into the *deserving* and the *undeserving* was also attributed to religious doctrines. Often cited was Paul's saying that "he who does not work, shall not eat" (2 Thessalonians 3.10). In the year 1216 Johannes Teutonicus wrote the *Glossa Ordinaria*, a commentary and gloss on an earlier religious codex; there he noted specifically that "the Church ought not to provide for a man who is able to work" (Tierney 1959:58). This division of the poor into those deemed worthy to receive help and those who should suffer because they were not deemed worthy was repeated for many centuries by the clergy and later by secular legislators and charity administrators, and also guided the approach to the poor in Colonial America. Cotton Mather (1663–1728), perhaps the most influential preacher in New England, urged his congregants to engage in "a perpetual endeavor to do good in the world," but at the same time warned them to support only those poor people who were worthy to receive their charity (1966).

Many liberal churchmen have been in the forefront of those who urged progressive legislation and more humane treatment for all who need help, but the stereotype that religion does not care for the helpless has remained prevalent and has contributed the lack of co-operation between social work and religion. Stereotypes, it should be remembered, are never wholly accurate, but need not be entirely inaccurate. Stereotypes do cause us to mistake causal connections; it is not the person's or institution's negative traits that cause our hostility, but rather our hostility causes us to characterize their traits as negative. Stereotypes about religion have led some social workers into active opposition to religion. For most social workers, this situation has re-sulted in an indifference and a lack of concern for all things religious, especially with respect to their professional practice.

Religious Institutions View Social Work

Just as there is no single social work response to religion, so is there no one view that can be said to characterize what religious people think about social work. Different religions and various religious leaders view social work from diverse perspectives and assess the profession's functions or dysfunctions in divergent ways. Many believers, including many members of the clergy, are among the strongest supporters of social work programs. They see no conflict between religion and social work. But there are others who do not view the activities of social workers so positively. Some, though supporting social work, decry the avoidance of all things spiritual in secular social work practice. Still others see in social work a threat which believers should avoid or even oppose.

The somewhat cool relationship between some of the clergy

and some social workers has been explained in different ways. There are those who attribute this to the fact that many members of the clergy devote a large part of their time and efforts to helping people cope with some of the very same problems for which social workers claim expertise. Four out of every ten American adults who have sought professional help for a personal problem turned to the clergy; 78 percent reported that the counseling they received from a member of the clergy had been helpful (Gurin, Veroff, and Feld 1960). Some priests, ministers, and rabbis refer people with serious problems to social workers or psychologists, but others feel that helping people who have problems is a legitimate and central part of their ministry. "The clergy are not doing anything they haven't done for 2000 years," said Kim Colby, an attorney who was defending one church in a million-dollar malpractice suit, filed by the parents of a man who had killed himself after receiving Bible counseling from the church's pastor. He added that "a church has the right to offer to help people by prayer and counseling based on the Bible." The judge evidently agreed with this argument and dismissed the case (*New York Times*, May 12, 17, 20, 1985).

Some ministers view social workers as competitors. They are especially concerned that nonreligious social workers provide help that they believe to be incompatible with the teachings of their church. They feel that it would be far better to let a person suffer and receive no help at all rather than be misled along ways that expose him or her to spiritual dangers. However, many others do not share these views. It has been said that all modern popes, from Pope Leo XIII to John Paul II, have so strongly supported and endorsed welfare efforts that for a Catholic to deny the value of social work would be close to heresy (Marty 1980:467). Many main-line Protestant ministers and almost all Jewish rabbis strongly support social work programs, even though they may not always be happy about what they consider to be social work's neglect of the religious aspects of problem situations.

Dealing with the Spiritual Malaise

Yet there are those among the clergy who are antagonistic to social workers and who think of them as cold, heartless, and irreligious, if not antireligious bureaucrats. Thus, at one church conference the chaplain discussed what it takes to help despondent persons; he contrasted the cold and unfeeling efforts of social workers with the warm approach of the clergy, which he said was filled with Christian love and understanding (Spencer 1956:19). Others have noted that as long as professional social work is based only on scientific and humanistic concepts, social workers will provide only superficial help. Real help, they argue, is given only when the helping process is based on religious principles. Another version of this proposition states that humanist social workers believe in man, while Christians believe in destiny (Keith-Lucas 1972:211). The basic problem, it is said, is that the humanist approach prevents social workers from dealing with the spiritual malaise that is one of the core problems of our age.

The gap between religion and scientific social work was recognized by many social workers very early in the development of the profession. One leader of the new profession characterized social work as "a revolutionary turning of thought in our society, from a religious service to God to a secular 'service to humanity' " (Huntington 1893, cited by Siporin 1975). It is no wonder that, given this approach, some of the clergy feared social work as a competitor for the loyalty of their members. This apprehension was reinforced by a widespread belief that professional social work was continuing to move toward a more intense and more radical secularism. Many saw in this development the creation of an unnatural schism between body and soul. When social work identified the satisfaction of individual desires as a high-priority professional goal, the gap between the professional and the religious approach became even wider. Again, it matters little whether these appraisals were accurate. To the extent that religious leaders believed that their views and perceptions reflected reality, these opinions colored their assessment of social workers, no matter what individual social workers might do or say.

For some ministers, especially for evangelicals, such as Dwight Moody (1837–1899) and Billy Sunday (1863–1935), a social worker's personal religious orientation was not important, since they opposed all social work efforts, believing that these distract from the church's real mission, which is to win souls. While their criticism was directed especially toward church social work programs, they also opposed nonsectarian social work programs because these permit or even encourage clients to continue to "live in sin." As far as they are concerned, any effort that does not contribute directly to the salvation of souls is a waste of time and must be opposed actively.

I have emphasized in the previous pages the opposition of some religious leaders to social work. However, it must be recognized that many believers, both among the clergy and the laity, have accepted nonsectarian secular social work as normative, just as they had earlier embraced nonsectarian public school education. Many clergy people serve on the boards of directors of social agencies. They refer church members to social workers for help, which they believe social workers are best equipped to provide. In summary, some members of the clergy reject social work, others are ambivalent, and still others support it. It can be said that the religious assessment of social work is hardly monolithic.

The Disjunction in Historical Perspective

As I stated earlier, the mistrust between social work and religion is a mutual one. To some it seems as if there is a brick wall between the Church and social work; before there can be any understanding and cooperation it will be necessary to build bridges to connect these two sectors. But others have noted that many joint social work–church programs and projects already exist. They believe that because of these there is no need for constructing new bridges (Howell-Thomas 1974). Though an understanding of the origins of the conflict between social work and religion may not fully explain its present significance, it may be helpful to inquire what brought about the current situation. A better understanding of the historical perspective may restore the balance and reduce the threats presented by the stereotypes prevalent on both sides.

The origin of almost all modern social services can be traced back to organized religion. The scope and extent of welfare services provided by the Church varied at different times and in different regions of the world, but whatever services existed (aside from the informal help provided by family and neighbors) were until modern times under the auspices or guidance of religious authorities. Even those scholars who date the secularization of charities several centuries earlier than

I do have noted the continued involvement of the clergy in welfare activities (Pullan 1976:19–21).

Johnson was correct when he observed that the Christian Church was "the mother of social work" (1941:404), but this does not mean that contemporary social work is based only or primarily on religious principles. Early in its history professional social workers found that religious sources did not provide them with the scientific theory base that they needed. This was one of the reasons why they abandoned religion and turned instead to other sources, principally to psychological and sociological theories.

To really understand the current relationship between social work and religion we must turn to a number of historical developments at the dawn of the modern era, starting with the fifteenth and sixteenth centuries. These, in time, had an enormous impact on the separation of social work from religion. They included the rise of the modern state, the rapid increase of rural poverty, the beginnings of the industrial revolution, and the Protestant Reformation. I shall briefly examine each of these developments and the implications for contemporary social work practice.

THE RISE OF THE MODERN STATE

Many scholars have noted the close connection between the rise of the modern state and the development of capitalism. By the middle of the fourteenth century medieval feudalism was rapidly losing its influence on events. The power of the feudal nobility was beginning to be replaced by that of a new business and industrial elite. Since trade could prosper only where security and order prevailed, there was almost everywhere a demand for replacing the small and weak feudal principalities with larger and stronger nation-states. In earlier times royalty and nobility had been dependent, more or less, on the approval or support of the Church, but the kings of these new nation-states amassed power and strength with the support and encouragement of the new commercial classes. As a consequence, the church's role as a societal center of strength and support became less and less important. Increasing conflict between the secular government and the previously powerful church became all but inevitable. These developments have many implications for the present discussion, but I will not trace them in detail. One example must suffice here. When Henry VIII of England evicted the religious communities from the monasteries and convents in 1536–39, he used this opportunity to strengthen his own power by distributing the expropriated properties among his friends and supporters. Though this royal initiative was not designed to affect the realm's social policy, it did put an end to one of the principal institutions for poor relief. Before long, the state had to assume some responsibility for the general welfare. This first tentative step in the assumption of responsibility by the secular authorities for emerging social problems set a crucial direction for England, as well as for the rest of Europe.

RURAL POVERTY AND VAGRANCY

A series of natural and man-made diseasters in western and central Europe so increased the problem of poverty at the beginning of modern times that the church, which traditionally took care of the poor, was no longer able to meet all of their needs. In the fourteenth century the Black Plague wiped out more than a third of Europe's population. In the following century landlessness increased in England and posed an ever more serious problem.

The plight of the rural dispossessed at the beginning of the sixteenth century is reminiscent of that of the many refugees in the last half of the twentieth century. Thomas More vividly portrayed their fate: "Away they trudge . . . out of their known and accustomed houses, finding no place to rest" (More 1922:33).

The vagrant poor were a problem not only in England but in almost every European country. People almost everywhere believed that domestic peace and tranquility were threatened by the constantly growing number of hungry vagrants. They enacted, therefore, anti-vagrancy legislation throughout the fifteenth century (DeSchweinitz 1972:30–38). No voluntary institution, not even the Church, was able to cope with so widespread a problem as vagrancy and poverty. The motivation of the state for reluctantly assuming responsibility for these problems was neither pity nor piety; instead, both the secular rulers and the business elite were convinced that "unrelieved and uncontrolled poverty was the most fertile breeding ground for local disorders" (Jordan 1959:77). Already at the dawn of the modern era, the need for self-protection and for system maintenance provided the major motivation for state intervention.

INDUSTRIAL REVOLUTION

The emerging social and economic order was based on an alliance between the business and industrial elites and the monarchs of the newly emerging centralized nation-states. This arrangement was essentially out of harmony with the social and economic ethics of the medieval Church. Aquinas had taught that every individual should be satisfied with his or her place in society, but the new ethic awarded a prize to those who were dissatisfied with their place in society and who, as a consequence, would lift themselves by their own efforts to higher positions. The vertical social structure where all persons knew their place and their relationship both to those above and to those below was replaced by a horizontal social structure that emphasized social class membership. The paternalism of the lord of the manor was replaced by cash wages, paid by the factory owner. The mechanical discipline of the machine replaced the pervasive authority of tradition. These changes occurred gradually between, the 16th and 19th centuries, but in time the Church was moved from a powerful central position to a weaker location on the sidelines of life.

PROTESTANT REFORMATION

The Protestant Reformation, according to the views of many, provided the intellectual and ideological framework for developments that later facilitated the near-universal acceptance of modern secularism and scientism. Luther's teachings that the church must maintain an uncritical attitude toward the secular state, since both Church and state were divinely established institutions, ultimately forced the Church into the shadow of the ever more powerful state. This, in turn, permitted the further development of science and scientism apart from the influence and control of the Church. Much later, a liberal Protestant theologian observed that the secularization of modern social work was largely the result of processes set in motion by the Protestant Reformation (Niebuhr 1932).

Secular Poor Relief Replaces Charity

The secular state's assumption of responsibility for poor relief and other social services was gradual and halting. For a long time the implementation was largely ineffective, but a fateful decision had been made when the responsibility for the poor was shifted from the Church to the state. Contemporary Protestant churches encouraged this development in many ways. Protestant clergy people, following the examples of Luther and Calvin, urged municipal or state authorities to cope with the growing economic and social problems faced by their citizens. Before long, under the influence of the Catholic Counter-Reformation, many Catholic clergy followed their example. Thus, the city fathers of Lyons, France, established in 1534 the Aumone-Générale, an institution designed to take care of the spreading "begging nuisance." Churches, monasteries, and benevolent citizens supported this public institution even though it was organized and operated by the secular authorities (Coll 1969:6; Pullan 1976).

While the seeds of the break between the religious and the secular delivery systems were already planted in the fifteenth and sixteenth centuries, the actual break was gradual and was not completed until the latter part of the nineteenth century. A number of societal developments, including the following, contributed to the final break:

INCREASED DIVISION OF LABOR

The principle of the division of labor was first proposed by the managers of the new factories. Greater availability of cheap power (including cheap human power) made it possible to expand the scope of production and manufacture. The older and more traditional production methods were no longer suitable for the new factories; they were soon replaced by newer ways, based (at first in a rudimentary way) on the principle of the division of labor. In time this principle spread from the factory floor to all other areas of life. Specialization became one of the hallmarks of the new age. The comprehensive, diffuse institutions of the past were now restricted so that their influence was felt in delimited areas only. The Church, perhaps the most comprehensive of all institutions in the premodern world, was no exception. The role of the clergy was redefined from that of community spiritual leaders with wide-ranging responsibilities in all areas of life to that of specialists in specific religious matters only.

This redefinition and limitation of the clergy's role evidently occurred in America long before it became common in Europe. De

Tocqueville observed as early as the 1830s that "in America religion is a distinct sphere, in which the priest is sovereign, but out of which he takes care never to go" (1954 2:28). Institutional areas for which the Church had carried responsibility for many centuries were transferred (wholly or in part) to other sectors—marriage and divorce to the state, education to public schools, and social services to nonsectarian welfare agencies. De Tocqueville's advice that religions would retain their authority only if "they confined themselves strictly within the circle of spiritual matters" was generally accepted by most but not all American churches (1954 2:24).

THE RISE OF SCIENTISM AND POSITIVISM

In the nineteenth century scientism became the dominant ideology throughout America. Scientism is the almost mystical belief that only science can provide the knowledge necessary for solving problems, technological as well as social and charitable. A reviewer of Deregando's *Visitor of the Poor* (1832) in the prestigious *North American Review* (January 1833, p. 111) wrote that the author attempted "to raise charity to the dignity of a science." "Scientific charity" was seen as the solution for all societal problems.

Mary Richmond is generally credited with introducing the scientific approach to casework practice in her pathbreaking book *Social Diagnosis* (1917), but a close reading of the proceedings of the annual meetings of the National Conference of Charities and Corrections reveals that the term "scientific social work" was already in frequent use before the turn of the century. Nor was Richmond the only social work educator who advocated a scientific approach. Arthur Todd of the University of Minnesota published his textbook *The Scientific Spirit of Social Work* (1920) only a few years after the appearance of Richmond's book. The fledgling social work profession fervently embraced the spirit of scientism, even while the churches, at least the more traditional and conservative ones, remained among the few social institutions that attempted to resist this trend.

COMPETITION FOR RESOURCES

The establishment of separate secular social service agencies resulted in a competition between them and the churches for funds, personnel, recognition, and acclaim. These resources are in limited supply. The first clash occurred around the competition for scarce personnel. Some people who were committed to the Church began to choose social work instead of church work. For example, Owen R. Lovejoy started life as a minister but later became a leading social work executive and social reformer. Jane Addams rejected a missionary career to become a pioneer social worker. The churches lost not only these two, but many others as well when people rejected organized religion and turned instead to social work (Marty 1980:477, 476). Later the competition for financial resources became a primary issue. For example, in 1981, 46 percent of all charitable funds were channeled to churches and religious institutions and were thus not available to nonsectarian, secular agencies; on the other hand, the churches failed to receive 54 cents out of every charitable dollar (Jacquent 1983:249).

STATISM

After the Napoleonic Wars, the consolidation and strengthening of the nation-states took on new urgency. It was not long before wise (or Machiavellian) statesmen saw the utility of public, nonsectarian welfare services as an instrument to assure the loyalty of the masses of urban workers to the state. Bismark's social security system was only the best known of several such efforts in Europe. Many of these developments occurred even before the new profession of social work was "born"; others took place during the early formative years of the profession so that the evolution of social work as a secular profession did not require any dramatic decisions but occurred quite naturally. The secular bent of the profession was evident even in America where governmental social services on the federal level did not develop until much later. Much of the initial inspiration for an American social work ideology came from England's settlement house and charity organization societies. The impact of continental social workers, such as Germany's Alice Solomon who was in regular contact with Mary Richmond and other American social work pioneers, has not yet been explored, but may also have been of significance.

The impact of each of these developments was uneven, but taken together they served to sharpen the disjunction between social work and religion and to provide a powerful base on which, in time, the structure of a secular social work profession was established.

The "Anachronism" of Religious Social Workers

Social work is generally thought of as a secular profession, but not all social workers are irreligious or indifferent religion. Some social workers are practicing and believing Christians, Muslims, or Jews. While there are no statistics that give accurate information about the number of religious social workers, few doubt that there are practitioners who have a deep religious commitment. Such social workers may be the exception to the rule, but the available data are so scarce that no definite statements can be made.

One Australian study, for example, compared social workers with psychologists and psychiatrists and found that social workers were more religious than members of the other two professions. Seventy percent of the psychiatrists and 69 percent of the psychologists reported that they held religious beliefs, while 81 percent of the social workers gave this response. Forty-two percent of the social workers reported that they prayed at least once a week, 50 percent reported that at some time in their life they had been in the presence of God (Cross and Khan 1983). Data from an earlier American study seem to corroborate these findings (Henry, Sims, and Spray 1971). The level of religiosity and irreligiosity among social workers may not differ greatly from that of the general population coming from the same socioeconomic group. However, clients often come from a different background than that of their social workers. This may result in a lack of congruence in religious beliefs and practices between workers and clients, a difference that deserves further attention.

Recently I discussed this problem of client worker differences with a group of social workers; one related that the social workers in her mental health center only recently became aware that they had completely overlooked the meaning that religion might have for their clients. She thought that the fact that all of the social workers in this agency were either secularist nonbelievers or atheists, while most of their clients were practicing believers, was the reason for this "oversight." The implications that such an oversight might have for practice will be discussed in a later chapter.

It is important to recognize that the crucial question is not whether to characterize all social workers or a particular practitioner as religious or irreligious, but how to deal with the dilemmas that may occur when a secular social worker is in contact with a religiously oriented client or when a religious social worker counsels a secular client.

In any event, the dichotomy of "secular" and "religious" social workers is probably an oversimplification. It may be more efficient to develop a model with three types, as follows:

Type 1: These social workers have no formal religious affiliation. They include a wide range of social workers who identify themselves as atheists, agnostics, or humanists, as well as ex-Christians, ex-Muslims, and ex-Jews who are now indifferent toward religion and have let lapse their membership in any formal religious group. A type 1 social worker may be as concerned with spiritual, ethical, and moral values as any other social worker, but he or she is not an active adherent to or member of any formal religious grouping.

Type 2: These social workers have maintained an affiliation with a religious group and accept, more or less, the obligations and rituals of that group, but they do not see any relevance of their religious beliefs for their professional practice. This felt lack of relevance may be the result of a weak commitment to or a low salience of religious beliefs (Moberg 1982). The pervasive acceptance of the "separation of church and state" doctrine tends to support the view that religion just is not relevant to the concerns of daily life. Yet, as I shall show later, the religious beliefs of this type of social worker may influence, unconsciously and unintentionally, their professional practice.

Type 3: These social workers are affiliated with a religious group and their entire life, including their professional practice, is guided by the tenets of that group. Most often these social workers are affiliated with a traditional or fundamentalist church or a cult.

Though I have presented a typology with three distinct types, the impact of religious values and beliefs on social work practice is not limited to these three alternatives. Instead, it might be more helpful to develop a model that considers the full range of the impact of religion on professional practice. In such a model, types 1 and 2 would occupy one extreme position, and type 3 the other extreme (figure 1.1). Social workers will be found all along this range, with only a relatively small number at either polar position. In other words, there are only a

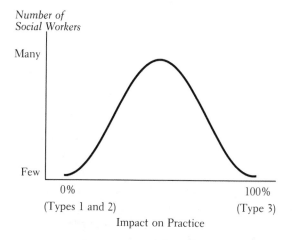

FIGURE 1.1. Impact of Religious Tenets on Practice: Hypothetical Distribution of Social Workers

relatively few social workers, if any, whose professional practice is influenced only by religious beliefs and values and by no other considerations, just as there are relatively few social workers whose professional practice is not influenced at all, either directly or indirectly, by any religiously derived values.

What difference does it make whether a social worker is more or less religious or not religious at all? Is not a person's religious beliefs that person's own personal business? The answers to these questions depend on whether religious beliefs influence the professional practice of social workers. This issue will be discussed at length in chapter 4.

Religion and Science Conflict

Radical secularists taught that the demise of religion was only a matter of time. Nietzche had already announced the death of God, but he also recognized that for the time being most people would continue to behave according to religious rules because they were afraid to live without them. Yet he and others were certain that in time all religions will disappear. If this view of the world is accurate, then the occasional religious social worker can be considered an anachronism, a member of a small group which will disappear before long.

Concern has been expressed that the inevitable conflict between science and religion would result in a religious social worker holding "two sets of fundamentally incompatible understandings of reality which could not be reconciled" (Judah 1985:26). This dilemma, it has been suggested, has contributed to the tension, even intolerance, between religious and secular social workers. Many secular social workers are convinced of the scientific superiority of atheism and believe that maturity requires putting aside such childish ideas as religion. This view has gained wide acceptance in professional circles. It may provide one explanation why religion has generally been ignored in the curriculum of schools of social work. The occasional social worker with strong religious identification was viewed as an anachronism by most teachers and colleagues.

But religion has not faded away. As American society has become at the same time more secular and more religious, there has been a renewed interest in religion. The number of religiously committed social work students and practititoners seems to have increased—not only in fundamentalist and denominational colleges that offer accredited social work programs, but throughout the profession. Numerically this may still be a small group, but what may have been the occasional anachronism of yesteryear has become an enigma in the profession. Many social work educators are puzzled because this type of social worker does not fit the professional model that they have constructed over the years. One indication of this concern was a special conference on "The Impact of Religious Fundamentalism on Social Work Education and Practice" (Cleveland State University, September 1985) which was convened to investigate the consequences of "the strong religious fundamentalist mood" for professional practice.

Chapter Two

Religion in the
Contemporary World

Many take it for granted that America is, or is rapidly becoming, a secular society where religion no longer plays an important role. Whatever religious activities remain have become peripheral to the concerns of life. Yet others suggest that the secularization process is no more than a metamorphosis of religion and that the "decline" really disguises a continuing religious impulse. The "death of religion" may have been celebrated prematurely.

Both the degree and the irreversibility of secularization may have been overestimated (Berger 1977:200). Indeed, many observers of American society speak of a reversal of the secular trend, and even of a "burgeoning religious revival" in the 1980s (Siporin and Glasser 1986; Yankelovich 1981). They say that the signs of this resurgence can be seen everywhere. But alongside these signs of a renewed religiosity there are also developments that give evidence of a continuing secularization; the clues are quite conflicting. If we are not careful, we will pay attention only to the information that will fit our preconceived biases. Such an approach, which ignores some data and perhaps puts false emphasis on other observations, is neither scientific nor helpful.

In this chapter I want to examine as carefully as possible the evidence available for the "religious revival" hypothesis, as well as the evidence that points to a continuing secularization. In order to better understand the place of religion in contemporary society, I will try to identify both the functions and dysfunctions that have been ascribed to religion. The traditional church/sect model will be utilized critically to deepen our understanding of religion in today's world. The functions filled by the cults that seem to abound everywhere will be noted. In short, I will try to introduce the reader to the multifaceted functions of religion in modern society.

Is There a Resurgence of Religion?

One of the dominant characteristics of life in the postmodern world is the resurgence of religion, according to Cox (1984). This assessment has been widely accepted, but we must also note the evidence of a continuing and ever-widening secularization process. Niebuhr's observation (1958) that "the United States has been at the same time one of the most secular and one of the most pious of modern societies" may still be valid today. Similar conclusions were drawn by Clebsch (1968), Marty (1980), and many others. Since the early days of the republic, the proportion of Americans attending church has been increasing steadily, though in the last generation there has been a decrease in religious activities of Catholics, Jews, and some Protestants. But a number of Protestant denominations, as well as some Jewish and Muslim religious groups, have shown remarkable gains in attendance and participation during the most recent period (Schroeder et al. 1974).

At the same time, values and norms that once seemed permanent have been widely abandoned with apparent ease. The eternal truths of yesterday have been replaced by scepticism and doubt. The forbidden has become commonplace and the exception the rule. In many communities it is "normal" to be irreligious or nonreligious, while the practicing believer has become almost marginal. Even many religious institutions seem to have become more and more secular. In such a society the polarization of positions that typified an earlier age may no longer be functional. Little is gained by applying to the total society such generalized labels as "more religious" or "more secular." Instead it is necessary to analyze the impact of religion and secularization on specific groups in the population. Such a review of the place and of the relevance of religion in our contemporary society may help us understand better the dilemmas that many society workers face in their professional practice.

Much of the debate about the recent resurgence of religion is based on impressions and "for example" arguments. There are few relevant statistics. Even reports from empirical research, while valuable, do not always lend themselves to generalizations. The finding that a cohort of college freshmen on one campus were "more religious" than were college freshmen on that campus ten years later is informative, but does not permit us to jump to conclusions about the state of religiosity in America or even on college campuses generally at the end of the twentieth century (Manese and Sedlacek 1983). Data derived from two thousand church members in seven suburbs of one Midwestern metropolitan community may provide many insights, but hardly permit generalizations about the religiosity of all Americans in the 1980s (Schroeder et al. 1974). This caution also applies to much of the material presented here.

Caplow, in the most recent Middletown study, paid particular attention to the religious practices and beliefs of the population of Muncie, Indiana (the location of the Middletown studies). He compared the church attendance of Middletown adults in 1977–78 with adult church attendance throughout the United States, as reported by a national sample which the National Opinion Research Center drew for its 1976 General Social Survey. Since an identical proportion of both groups reported regular church attendance, he suggested that it was safe to generalize U.S. religious patterns from the Muncie data. However, the situation is not quite that simple, since a significantly higher proportion of Middletown adults never attended church than was true for the national sample population (Caplow et.al. 1982:387). This does not necessarily mean that Middletown adults were less religious than most Americans. Rather it suggests the difficulties of deducing accurate conclusions for the total population from specific one-group survey data.

Caplow et al. (1982) also observed that contemporary Middletowners are far more tolerant of other religions, even of non-Christian and non-Western religions, than were their fathers and grandfathers. But this spirit of tolerance is not an entirely new phenomenon. It has always characterized Americans and has distinguished American culture from its European sources.[1] De Tocqueville (1954) noted more

1. Admittedly, the countervalue of intolerance has also characterized American life. Since the

than 150 years ago that American society, in contrast to European society, was characterized by a spirit of pluralism which permitted the existence, side by side, of many different religions. Initially only Protestant denominations were tolerated. Later, this tolerance was extended to Catholics and, still later, also to Jews and Muslims. Today even those without religion benefit from this spirit of tolerance.

Yet there are limits beyond which many Americans are not ready to go. Nine out of every ten Americans said that they would support a Catholic candidate for the presidency, and eight out of ten were ready to vote for a Jewish candidate, but less than half of the respondents thought that they would cast their ballot for a candidate who was an atheist (Gallup 1980:99). Nevertheless, Americans have come a long way from the days when those who were not Christians were considered to be beyond the social pale. This spirit of tolerance is indigenous to American life and should not be taken as evidence of any weakening of religious authority or of a growing secularism.

Rugged Individualism and Self-Fulfillment

This same culture, which has stressed tolerance, has also fostered and rewarded rugged individualism. Though this is most generally associated with the pioneer days of America's westward expansion and with the days of the "robber barons," it is still considered important today, though it has been transformed somewhat to make it more consistent with the demands of modern times. The same ideology that gave legitimacy to rugged individualism has also legitimized the quest for self-fulfillment and has provided the intellectual and cultural backing for the contemporary emphasis placed on the individual and on the rights of individuals. Recent research suggests that "the rage for self-fulfillment . . . has spread to virtually the entire U.S. population." Seven out of every ten Americans are spending "a great deal of time" thinking about themselves and about their inner life while not thinking

---

days of the Massachusetts Puritans, when nonconformists like Roger Williams were expelled and Salem witches were burned, until our own days when discrimination against women and gays and blacks and other minorities is still rampant, intolerance has never been entirely eliminated. Yet in contrast with other countries, American society appears more tolerant.

much about the general welfare or about their community (Yankelovich 1981:5).

This self-centeredness is also evident in the religious sphere.
While a growing number of Americans said that religion is playing a
greater role in society, their faith is essentially self-centered. Religious
beliefs and activities are more often justified in terms of "it makes me
feel good" than in terms of the need to do God's will (Gallup 1985:12–
13). This fixation on the self may be an indication of a sick society.
Some claim that this preoccupation has damaged the social fiber of
American society—that the "radical individualism" may have grown
cancerous. This "cancer" has rendered many in America's middle class
incapable of expressing a commitment to such basic institutions as
marriage, family, and religion (Bellah et al. 1985). There are also those
who caution that this "individualistic autonomy [is] counterproductive
in a society that needs much more collaborative collectives and in-
terdependent, normative relationships and conduct" (Siporin and Glasser 1987:220). As long as rugged individualism was part of a belief
system that also included the family and the Church, it motivated
people to excel and advance (though too often without taking into
consideration the social costs that others had to pay). But when the
value of rugged individualism becomes the key motif of a generation
that is skeptical about all belief systems, it can be perilous. People
who no longer believe in anything outside of themselves may also lose
faith in themselves and in their own abilities.

This pervasive lack of meaning was particularly evident in the
post-Vietnam period. For many, the ideals of democracy, equality,
and freedom lay shattered. But life without meaning, sooner or later,
becomes boring or unbearable. When neither science and rationalism,
nor traditional values and religious beliefs, are able to give meaning
to life, people will turn to other sources for meaning. Some turned to
drugs, others to alcohol. Some tried one or more of the many esoteric
cults. Still others answers turned to fundamentalist sects. Many reex-
plored the traditional values and religious beliefs that their parents or
grandparents had jettisoned when they entered the modern age. Some
tried all of these ways in sequence. There are those who interpret this
search for meaning, a search that is often accompanied by increased
religious activity, as a resurgence of religion in American life. It has
even been cited as a proof for Hansen's Law, which states that "what

the son wishes to forget, the grandson wishes to remember" (Hansen 1952).

Popularity of Cults

Esoteric cults, many derived from or associated with non-Western faith ideologies, have become popular among many of those who did not find satisfactory answers in their own tradition. The complete break with the family of origin and with the previous way of life that many cults demand tends to facilitate the adaptive process to the value system of the new cult. To some outsiders this process may seem akin to brainwashing, but for the believer it is precisely this total immersion that again gives meaning to life (Gordon 1984). This search for meaning along nontraditional lines is not limited to the members of any one social class. Many have noted that it is particularly evident among the children of the affluent middle class, the very class that, according to Bellah et al. (1985), is most affected by the "cancer" of rugged individualism. However, cults today number among their members the rich, the poor, and those in between. They meet a particular need for America's dispossessed minorities, including blacks, Hispanics, and recent immigrants. For many in these groups, the intimacies and direct experiences offered by small sects and cults serve as a secure haven in a world of unrest.

Esoteric cults represent one way of searching. Fundamentalist religion is another. While membership in main-line Protestant churches decreased between 1973 and 1981, fundamentalist churches reported marked gains. Membership in the Southern Baptist Convention was up by 15 percent, in the Church of Jesus Christ of Latter-Day Saints by 40 percent, and in the Assemblies of God by 71 percent (Gallup 1985:11). This upsurge in fundamentalism has occurred not only in Christendom but in all parts of the world. Egypt's Muslim Brotherhood and Iran's Khomeniism are only two of many examples of fundamentalist expansion in the non-Western world. The turning from atheism, agnosticism, secularism, and liberal religion to traditionalism and fundamentalism is the result of a pervasive disillusionment with the unfulfilled promise of rationalism and humanism. One student of the American religious scene observed that this reversal of the secularization process may be due to "the pervasive boredom of a world without gods" (Berger 1977:201).

Religion is not the only sector that has witnessed a move to the "right," to a more traditional way of life. Suddenly it has become fashionable to express views that are neither liberal nor radical. For the first time in several generations conservative policies have found wide public acceptance. President Reagan's election in 1980 and 1984 was generally attributed to the growing acceptance of the conservative point of view. The dismantlement of the welfare state almost everywhere gives evidence of this trend in the political sphere. The seeming about-face of Congress and the courts on the abortion issue is part of the same trend. The gradual return of prayer to the public schools also reflects this mood. Many churches, even liberal churches, have reported a similar move to the right. The Roman Catholic Church's virtual abandonment of many of the policies promulgated during the Second Vatican Council is another example of this trend.

The various bits of evidence presented so far tend to support the view that there has been a resurgence of religion in American life. But "more religion" does not yet inform us about the role that religion fills in contemporary society. This I will attempt to explore in the next section.

The State of Religion in Secular Society

There may be more religious activity in America today than there was a generation ago—or there may be less. What difference does this really make? How important is organized religion nowadays? How relevant is it to the major concerns of society?

How we define religion is important. Marx (1963:43–4) called religion "the opium of the people," while Durkheim (1954:12) considered it "a basic integrative mechanism." Weber (1963:33) thought of religion as "a source of social and cultural patterns," but Lenin (1940:11) charged that it was "a form of oppression." For Freud religion was only the recapitulation of the infantile, "born of the need to make tolerable the helplessness of man" (1928:28–32). Shils wrote that religious beliefs satisfy the "universal need for contact with sacred values" (1968:748).

The word *religion* comes from the Latin *religiare*, which means to bind together. Originally religion was used in the sense of binding humans to God, but quite early an additional function was assigned to religion—to bind human beings together in society (Coughlin 1965). Traditionally the term *religion* has been used to identify faith groups (for example, Christianity, Islam), buildings used for worship (chapel, synagogue), worship ritual and the recitation of specific prayers (baptism, Holy Communion), as well as the adherence to sanctified doctrines and beliefs (Apostles' Creed, Westminster Confession).

William James, one of the first psychologists concerned with the question of religion, indicated that there is no one emotion that can be identified as religious, but that instead there are a wide set of experiences that focus on a religious object. While James may have exaggerated by recognizing an almost unlimited variety of emotions as religious, this view is not uncommon among modern psychologists (Allport 1950). For James, religion meant "the feelings, acts, and experiences of individual men in their solitude, so far as they apprehend themselves to stand in relation to whatever they may consider divine" (1936:31–32). By emphasizing the experiential James taught that every religious experience, and especially every mystical experience, has a sense of immediacy (1936:371). Soloveitchik, coming from a different religious tradition, emphasized the cognitive and the intellectual in addition to the experiential. "Religious experience is not only of emotional or ethical essence, but is also deeply rooted in the noetic sphere." According to Solveitchik, "the urge for *noesis* is of the very essence of religion" (1986:3).

Broad or Narrow Definition of Religion

There are some contemporary writers who have used the term "religion" in a very broad way. Luckman, for example, extended the definition "beyond the bounds of the traditional creeds and institutions" to include all of a person's serious concerns that transcend the strictly biological. He defined this "invisible religion" as "the sacred cosmos" and "the ultimate meanings" felt by most persons, even by those not strongly attached to any traditional church (1967:102). According to this definition, a person need never attend church nor practice any of the rituals of a formal religion, need not even accept a church's doctrines and ethical codes, yet can be considered religious.

The problem with such broad definitions is that they make it difficult, if not impossible, to assess the state of religiosity of a given society or of a specific group in that society at any given point in time. Maslow reported that he once shared a platform with theologian Paul Tillich who defined religion as "concern with ultimate concerns." Maslow, an avowed secular humanist, defined humanistic psychology in the identical way and then wondered whether there was really any difference between a supernaturalist and a humanist (1970:45). Or, to use our terminology, given such a broad definition, what is the difference between a religious person and a secular person? If almost everything qualifies as religion, there is no point in saying that some persons are more religious than others, or that people today are more religious (or less religious) than they were a generation ago.

I will opt for a narrower definition of religion, but one that is broad enough to include all formal faith groups, even those nontraditional, non-Western cults and sects that have proliferated in contemporary American society. I will define a person as religious if he or she belongs to a faith group, accepts the beliefs, ethics, values, and doctrines of that group, and participates in the required activities, ceremonies, and rituals of the chosen group. (For other examples of multidimensional definitions of religion, see King 1967; Lenski 1961; and Stark and Glock 1970.) My definition of religion does not deny the possibility of an individual (or of a group) having a deep commitment to spiritual or religious values without having a formal affiliation with a religious institution and without practicing any recognized religious rituals. Such a person need not be an atheist, not even irreligious, but in the sociological sense he cannot he defined as a religious person.

Social Functions of Religion

Many of those who in their own lives no longer value religion agree that in earlier times religion filled important societal functions. But they note that in modern society religion is no longer relevant. Positivists, following the teachings of Comte, suggest that religion is no longer a force that makes for stability in human society. While Comte recognized that religion had made an important contribution to the early development of society, his famous "Law of the Three Stages" predicted that eventually science would replace religion completely. Following in Comte's footsteps, the American sociologist Kingsley Davis wrote that religion was patently false, but that it persists because it is still socially valuable; he, like so many others, had no doubt, however, that before long religion would disappear altogether (1948:509–48).

Durkheim, one of the early giants of French sociology, was among the first of modern sociologists to free himself from the influence of Comte's positivist philosophy. In his seminal *Elementary Forms of Religious Life* (1912) he identified the *conscience collective* as the essential connection between religion and social order. Religion, according to Durkheim, continues to play a crucial and positive role in the maintenance of the social system. If there were no such institution as religion, society would need to invent it. Many students of the sociology of religion have followed Durkheim's lead. Yet the Durkheimian method of studying religion, with its emphasis on structural functions, valuable as it is, may fail to convey the full meaning of religious experiences. For the believer, religion is much more than merely a means for social integration. Durkheim himself knew this, but those who followed him did not always pay sufficient attention to his observation that most believers object to the rational way of analyzing religion since "they feel that the real function of religion is not to make us think, to enrich our knowledge, . . . but rather it is to make us act, to aid us to live" (1954:416).

The influence of Weber on the American sociology of religion was relatively small because most of his major works on religion did not become available in American translations until the 1950s and 1960s. An exception was his *Protestant Ethic and the Spirit of Capitalism*, which had already appeared in translation in 1930. In this book Weber traced the close connection between economic and societal transformations, on the one hand, and ethical and religious changes, on the other. Following the tradition of German phenomenologists, Weber demanded that religious experiences and religious symbols be viewed in terms of those who believed in them and not on the basis of some "objective" criteria. His interest was not in the beliefs themselves but in the consequences that beliefs had for people who accepted them.

But we need to go beyond these positions if we wish to really understand the place of religion in modern society. We must try to understand the functions and dysfunctions of religion both for the individual believer and for society as a whole. Contemporary scholars have examined religion just as they have studied other social institutions. They have identified a number of different *functions*, including the following:

1. Religion serves an integrative function by establishing norms and values, making for moral character and for ethical relations with others.

2. Religion serves a social control function by fostering order, discipline, and authority.

3. Religion provides the individual believer with emotional support when needed.

4. Religion confers on believers a sense of identity.

5. Religion can serve as a source of positive mental health. It can contribute to happier, more stable families, marriages, and communities.

At the same time, a number of *dysfunctions* have been identified, including the following:

1. Religion may promote fanaticism, intolerance, and prejudice.

2. In a pluralistic society, religion no longer serves an integrative function, but has become a socially disruptive force, dividing society into believers and nonbelievers.

3. Religion, directly or indirectly, supports the establishment by directing attention away from social injustices. In this way it tends to perpetuate these injustices.

Not every scholar accepts this exact list of functions and dysfunctions. Some have reservations about the accuracy of this or that point. Others raise the more general question whether in contemporary society there still is any functional importance for organized religion.

Allport, for example, questioned the proposition that there is a direct and positive relationship between religion and prejudice. He suggested on the basis of his research that the crucial variable related to prejudice is the quality of the religious commitment, not the mere religious identification. Those who are "intrinsically religious," that is, people who use religion for obtaining personal security and peace of mind, may be prejudiced and may score relatively high on racist feelings. On the other hand, there are those who associate religion with a concern for others; their religious feelings are based on deep spiritual motivations. These people are "extrinsically religious" and are much less likely to be prejudiced and racist. Most racist of all are those who are "indiscriminately religious," that is, people who score high both on the intrinsic and on the extrinsic religious scale (Allport 1966; Allport and Ross 1967).

Evidence of Continuing Secularization

In their examination of the place of religion in American life, Glock and Stark questioned the relevance of religion in today's world. They observed that "organized religion at present is neither a prominent witness to its own value system nor a major focal point around which ultimate commitments to norms, values and beliefs are formed" (1965:184). Berger noted a quarter of a century ago that "an objective observer is hard put to tell the difference (at least in terms of values affirmed) between church members and those who maintain an 'un-churched' status" (1961:41). In 1973, only 28 percent of college youths and 42 percent of noncollege youths rated religion as a very important value, while the overwhelming majority of all youths disvalued religion (Yankelovich 1974:14, 26).

Heresy and religious apathy have been known throughout recorded history, but the prevalence of a religionless culture in which it is normative to be nonreligious or irreligious is characteristic only of modern times. Many people, even those who in their personal lives follow the precepts of religion, take it for granted that America is, or is rapidly becoming, a secular and pluralistic society where religion no longer plays an important role. The pronouncement of the "death of God" has been widely accepted. Even believers have reconciled themselves to the fact that they are in a minority and that for the majority, God no longer matters.

Evidence can be presented that "proves" the lack of relevance of religion in contemporary society, just as other data document the continued vitality of religion. Here are some random examples that demonstrate religion's "lack of relevance":

• Religion no longer provides an authoritative guide for daily life. The nonrelevance of the Church as a social control agent has been accepted by many church members, even by many clergy people. In a study of suburban congregations, the majority of all lay respondents did not agree with the statement that churches (or synagogues) should enforce a strict standard of moral conduct among their members. This also was the position of a large proportion of the clergy. Only 40 percent of Roman Catholic priests and only 6 percent of the Protestant ministers affiliated with the National Council of Churches of Christ (NCC) agreed that the churches should enforce strict moral standards among their members. A larger proportion of the more conservative and fundamentalist Protestant ministers agreed with the statement, but even among this group 43 percent thought that social control was no longer a function of the contemporary Church (Schroeder et al. 1974:72, 179–80).

• Despite strong prohibitions against sexual relations before marriage by most religious authorities, the proportion of women who delay sexual relations until marriage declined from 48 percent among those who married in the early 1960s to 21 percent among those who married in the late 1970s (National Center for Health Statistics 1985). Four out of every five women who marry now do not pay attention to Church teachings prohibiting premarital sex. The occasional attempts to persuade teenagers not to engage in sex almost never emphasize the religious or ethical aspects of this behavior. Motivated by a growing concern about the increasing number of teenage pregnancies or by the fear of AIDS or sexually transmitted diseases (STDs), the appeal is usually utilitarian. Thus, Ann Landers (1986) wrote in her nationally syndicated column, "There's a big campaign on urging kids to say no. I think it's great, but I am aware once you've said yes it's not likely you'll say no." Even some of the clergy have adopted this utilitarian approach. For example, the media gave wide coverage to a Unitarian minister who distributed condoms to church members during a sermon on avoiding sexually transmitted diseases (*Boston Globe,* February 9, 1987, p. 40).

• No statistics are available on the incidence of incest, yet the prestigious Sex Information and Education Council published an article by James Ramey in which he wrote that "we are in roughly the same position today regarding incest as we were a hundred years ago with respect to our fear of masturbation" (cited by Will 1980). No Christian church and almost no other religious group allows any exceptions to this "last taboo." Yet the reported incidence of incest is growing year after year. Will Church teachings in this area also be ignored as have been its teachings in most other areas of human behavior? This idea is not as farfetched as it may appear to some. Already there are groups that advocate early incestual sexual indoctrination in order to ensure positive sexual attitudes among children (Star 1980).

• The proportion of Americans attending religious services in any given week has been declining since the mid-1950s. In 1955, 49 out of every 100 American adults reported that they had attended a church or synagogue in the preceding seven days. By 1984, this figure had declined to 40 percent (Gallup 1985:42). However, some denominations, particularly conservative and fundamentalist churches, have reported increasing attendance.

• There does not seem to be any less crime or delinquency among religious people than among the nonreligious. Neither church affiliation, church attendance, nor belief in God seems to be significantly related to delinquency (Hirschi and Stark 1969). But there does seem to be somewhat less alcohol and drug abuse among religious people (Higgins and Albrecht 1977).

• The traditional Sabbath rest from work on Sundays has all but disappeared for most Americans. Suburban shopping malls draw more customers on Sundays than on any other day of the week. Sports, recreational activities, and meetings fill the time that once was devoted to worship or family devotions.

• The mass media, especially television, constantly focus on the lack of importance of religion in contemporary life. Many devout Christians have accepted this stereotyped picture of reality and regard themselves as exceptions, even when they are surrounded by people who believe like themselves (Caplow 1983).

TABLE 2.1. Church/Synagogue Membership,
1937–1984
(Percent of U.S. Adult Population)

1937	73%
1942	75
1947	76[a]
1952	73
1965	73
1975	71
1977	70
1982	67[b]
1983	69
1984	68

Source: Gallup 1985:40
[a]high point
[b]low point

Evidence of Religious Vitality

Yet there is also evidence that suggests the continuing vitality of religion in American life.

• A series of survey studies report that nearly all Americans subscribe to a code of morality derived from Jewish and Christian sources. Ninety-four percent say that they believe in God, 88 percent say that the Bible is the inspired word of God, 90 percent identify themselves with a specific denomination, church, or synagogue, and 89 percent say that they pray regularly (Neuhaus 1985:43).

• The people of Middletown (Muncie, Indiana) are more religious today than they were in the 1920s and 1930s when the Lynds undertook their well-known survey of life in this typical mid-America community. In 1924, 53 percent of Middletown married women reported that they never attended church; only 17 percent gave this response in 1978. In 1924, only 23 percent attended church regularly, but 48 percent reported that they did so in 1978 (Caplow et al. 1982:385). Caplow, as I noted already, thinks that it is reasonable to generalize the Muncie findings to all of contemporary American society.

• Seven out of every ten American say that they are members of a church or a synagogue. This proportion has remained more or less constant in the past fifty years, varying by no more than +/− five percentage points (see table 2.1).

• The religious revival seemed to continue in the late 1970s and 1980s, after a slight "cooling-off"period in the early 1970s. A particularly high religious consciousness and level of participation has been noted in recent years among teenagers, tomorrow's adults. Comparing Catholic adolescents with Catholic young adults in Canada and the United States, Greeley reported that 68 percent of the teens, but only 37 percent of the young adults, attend mass almost every week (1981:147). Admittedly, others interpret this data quite differently: today's adolescents will behave like today's young adults when they become young adults, thus supporting the secularization hypothesis.

• Religious observances and religious beliefs are still among the most significant factors that make for happy families and stable marriages, according to the findings of at least one recent study (Filsinger and Wilson 1984).

• People with religious faith seem to be able to cope better with disaster, injury, and serious illness than those without faith (Frank 1978).

• Although Americans engage in a wide variety of secular activities on Sundays, three out of every four say that this day has a particular religious or spiritual meaning for them. While 53 percent report that they work around the house on Sunday and 19 percent go shopping on that day, 54 percent attend church and 19 percent read the Bible (Gallup 1980:30).

• The resurgence of conservative political views may reflect an abiding religious commitment by most Americans. The campaign to restore traditional moral and spiritual values in public life may more accurately reflect the ideology of the majority of Americans than did the libertarian public and legal decisions of the 1960s and the 1970s. The drive to restore prayer and Bible readings in public schools, the attempts to overrule *Roe v. Wade* and to limit abortions, and the efforts to restrict pornography reflect, according to many analysts, the basic religious mold of the American people, today as always.

Dysfunctions of Religious Pluralism

The lack of official statistics on religious affiliation makes it difficult to speak with any accuracy about the changing importance of religion in America. The strong and vehement objection of several religious groups to the government's asking questions about religion has kept such questions out of the U.S. Census and out of the Current Population Survey (CPS). Only once, in March 1975, was one question on religion included in the CPS, but because of loud objections by many, this question was not repeated in subsequent surveys. As a result, most researchers have depended on the findings of national surveys, such as those conducted regularly by the National Opinion Research Center and the Gallup Surveys on Religion. The findings of various surveys have not always been consistent and have been used to support different positions.

Another difficulty in analyzing the impact of religion in modern society is that the religious experience is neither a homogeneous nor a monolithic phenomenon. One cannot speak of *the* Catholic view on most social questions. It is not possible to define a unitary Christian view on society. And it is quite impossible to ascertain what religious people in general think on any particular matter. A liberal theologian may encourage or tolerate the very same behaviour that a more traditional clergy person has pronounced a major sin. It is this situation that makes it unclear whether one can take behaviors such as the increase in premarital sex or abortion as indicators of the decreasing impact of religion. D'Antonio and Stact (1980) suggested, for example, that the increasing support for the right to abortion throughout the American population does not necessarily represent a rejection of religion, but rather a reevaluation of traditional values in the light of changing conditions.

The religious pluralism, characteristic of American society, also creates a situation where religious norms appear as ambiguous, vague, and even contradictory. One of the major findings of the most recent Middletown study was the growing tolerance for other beliefs, even for non-Christian beliefs, as well as for nonbelief, together with a continued adherence to traditional Christian theology (Caplow et al. 1982, Caplow 1983). Cuddihy called this phenomenon "the Protestant etiquette, a ritualized belief that no religion should offend another" (1978). This religious pluralism had earlier been identified as a major value of American democracy (Bellah and Hammond 1980). Religious pluralism is usually presented as a very positive feature of American society, but those who want to understand American life must also consider possible dysfunctions of this value.

Many of the societal functions assigned to religion are weakened when religious pluralism prevails. While the secular law is clearly codified and gives the impression of being definite, the multiplicity of religious "positions" tends to confuse the average person. When religious norms are ambiguous while the secular law is clear, people tend to follow the latter (Wuthnow 1979:25). Even members of the clergy may find it difficult to tell which is the "right" way. Just over half of the non–NCC-affiliated Protestant ministers in Schroeder's study of suburban congregations agreed that it was wrong for a woman to have an abortion under any circumstances in the first three months of pregnancy, but an almost equal number (48 percent) did not think that this was necessarily wrong (1974:79). In these circumstances, the secular law that unequivocally permits abortions during the first trimester tends to guide most people's behavioral choices.

However, when religious values are communicated clearly, religiously committed people do respond differently than those not so committed. This may explain the findings of a Canadian national survey which reported that those who never attend church are far more likely to approve abortions for economic and social reasons than those who attend church regularly every week (see table 2.2). Seventy percent of regular church attenders evidently feel that the church permits abortion of a defective fetus or that the message on this case is not clear. However, when it comes to the question of abortion for social and economic reasons, 70–80 percent of churchgoers in this sample were opposed. Evidently, the church's message opposing abortion is now clear and unambiguous for this group.

Churches and Sects in Modern America

In the sociology of religion, the church/sect typology has been of central importance.[2] It has helped many to clarify variations in different re-

2. This typology is generally ascribed by American sociologists to Ernst Troeltsch because his *Die Soziallehren der christlichen Kirchen und Gruppen* (Tübingen: Mohr, 1912) appeared in America in an English translation in 1931. Max Weber also made extensive use of the church/sect typology. Though an English translation of his *Die protestantische Ethik und der Geist des Kapitalismus* (1904 05, reprinted in *Gesammelte Aufsätze zur Religionssoziologie*, Tübingen:

TABLE 2.2. Attitudes on Abortion

Percent of Canadians Who Agree that a Woman Should be Able To Obtain a Legal Abortion:	Weekly Church Attenders	Never Attend Church
If there is a strong chance that the fetus is defective	70%	97%
If the family cannot afford any more children	31	81
If she does not want to marry the child's father	25	74
If she does not want any more children	19	75

Source: adapted from Bibby 1983

ligious institutions. Yet several contemporary analysts have questioned the usefulness of this typology for understanding American religious groups. I will examine their objections after first explaining the characteristics of church-type and sect-type institutions.

The church/sect typology is based on the proposition that these two types emphasize different aspects of religion and therefore require qualitatively different commitments from their adherents. The church type, according to Troeltsch (1931 1: 331–43) and others, typically has the following characteristics:

1. Churches are usually conservative (in the sense of not encouraging radical life-style changes).

2. The membership of any given church tends to be large.

3. Membership in a church is generally based on birth, though others may join by undergoing a conversion ritual.

4. Formal dogmas specify the officially approved beliefs. Church law clearly outlines the procedures governing all internal and external procedures.

5. Hierarchically appointed (or sanctioned) officials administer the means of grace, conduct the religious service, and fill other spiritual functions.

6. The social structure of churches is generally open, tends to be universal, and often coincides with geographic or ethnic boundaries.

7. The Church accepts the secular order and weaves it into its own life. It tends to support and reinforce secular societal values.

Mohr, 1920) appeared in England in 1930, it evidently did not reach America until after Troeltsch's name had already become associated with the church/sect typology. Weber noted that this typology "has been used at about the same time and, I assume, independently from me, by Kattenbusch. . . . Troeltsch accepts it and discusses it more in detail" (Weber 1958:255 *n*). Parsons was aware of Weber's earlier use of this typology and refers to the Weber-Troeltsch distinction of church and sect (1961:645).

These are the characteristics that make it possible for the Church "to receive the masses and to adjust itself to the world" (Troeltsch 1931 2:993).

The sect type, on the other hand, features other characteristics, including the following:

1. Membership in a sect is not automatic by birth but requires a voluntary commitment, usually a spiritual conversion (being "born again").

2. A sect is typically small in order to permit direct personal fellowship among the members.

3. For the sect members, a literal interpretation of the Scriptures reveals the complete and exclusive religious truth, and provides the framework and guidelines for all areas of human affairs. Sanctions are imposed on members whose behavior contravenes the sect's strict code.

4. Religious leaders, if any, are generally selected or elected from within the local laity; if there is a hierarchy, it is of the "flat" type with very few hierarchal levels. Religious obligations apply equally to all members.

5. The sect's social structure tends to be closed and exclusive, emphasizing the difference between the "saved" and the "sinners."

6. Religious experiences are viewed as alternatives to the secular life of the general society. Withdrawal from, indifference toward, or defiance of the world, its institutions, and its values are emphasized. Dual allegiance to religion and to the world is not permitted or is severely discouraged.

7. The sect members' way of life is characterized by an ethical austerity, and is often ascetic in nature.

The sect is a "voluntary society, composed of strict and definite Christian believers, bound to each other by the fact that all have experienced the 'new birth' " (Troeltsch 1931 2:448; see also Wilson 1982:89–93). Sect-type religious organizations also occur in non-Christian religions.

The Sacred and the Profane

Church and sect respond differently to what Durkheim posed as one of the major problems of our day—the relationship between the sacred and the profane. How do people relate the sacred and the profane aspects of their life? How do they divide their time between the demands of religion and of the secular life? Adherents of the church type of religion solve this problem by a pattern of alternations: short periods of religious celebration or observance are interspersed among lengthy periods of work and other secular pursuits.

Over the centuries, the time allocated to religious celebrations has become shorter and shorter. In the sixteenth century, according to Sombart (1915), fewer than two out of every three days were available for work, with the balance reserved for feasts, fasts, and other religious observances which made secular pursuits impossible. In one German town, 80 out of 208 days were observed as holy days; in another town, 62 out of 161 days were devoted to religious observances, while in a third, 94 of 287 days required religious obligations that made work impossible. There is no reason to believe that this situation was limited to Germany. Similar statistics can be amassed for nearly every other European country.

In Puritan Boston, people crowded into church every Thursday morning to hear the word of God. When it became obvious that these religious lessons brought about the loss of a whole day of work, the Court of Assistants ordered that no public lecture begin before one o'clock in the afternoon so that the Boston townspeople would work at least half a day. Ten years later, in 1645, the legislature asked the elders of the Boston church "to consider about the length and frequency of church assemblies" because these had resulted in "the great neglect of their affairs and the damage of the public." Although the elders indignantly denounced the magistrates's interference in religious matters, before long the number of church services was reduced and their length shortened (Rutman 1965:109, 259).

Over the centuries the time devoted to religion was decreased, while the days allocated to work activity was increased. The mechanization that accompanied the industrial revolution placed a premium on continual production, even while the wage economy made it prohibitive to devote too much time to religious observances. Today members of church-type religious groups usually allocate only a few hours per week to religious activities. One hundred and fifty years ago de Tocqueville recommended that religious observances and obligations be kept few in number and be limited to those that are absolutely necessary. He warned that "a religion which became more insistent in details, more inflexible, and more burdened with small observances . . . would soon find itself limited to a band of fanatic zealots in the midst of a sceptical multitude" (1954 2:26).

We still feel the pressure to reduce the number of nonwork days to a minimum. The observances of Lincoln's Birthday and Washington's Birthday were combined into one national holiday because two holidays in February were thought to be too much. Similarly, in most industrialized countries official national holidays generally are limited to no more than one a month. There are nine national holidays in the United States, eleven in France, twelve in Japan, and fifteen in West Germany (Swissair 1985).

Members of the sect-type religious groups solve the problem of the relation of the sacred and the profane in an entirely different way. They do so by practicing a pattern of interpenetration. Instead of allocating specific times and places to religious activities and others to secular activities, they attempt to merge the two spheres. The same rules and norms govern their behavior at work and in church, so that there is no clear separation between the religious and the secular. They do not limit prayer, for example, to a specific time or place, but consider that it is desirable and effective at all times, everywhere.

Adherents of the church-type religion have no great difficulty in separating different aspects of their lives. On the job they are workers, while in church they are worshippers. Different rules, even different norms, may govern their behavior at work and in church. The devout church worshiper may be a tyrant in the corporate office. The minister's sermon on Sunday is believed to be irrelevant to the business decisions that must be made on Monday. Those adhering to a sect-type religion are appalled by what they regard to be a schizophrenic approach, but most church-type people do not see their behavior in this light.

Limitations of the Church/Sect Typology

Several contemporary writers have questioned the appropriateness of the church/sect typology for the United States (for example Niebuhr

1958; Schroeder et al. 1974; Yinger 1970). In traditional European societies, sects characteristically arose as radical protests against the established church. But in the United States, where there is no established church, a large number of new religious groups emerge each year.[3] These may be more conservative or more innovative than the parent religious group from which they split or which they try to supplant. Over time these protest groups become institutionalized and take on more and more of the characteristics of the American denomination, a type that some consider to be an intermediate between church and sect. This institutionalization process becomes even more evident in the second and subsequent generations when membership is generally derived by birth rather than by voluntary affiliation. For example, today almost all members of such "sects" as the Amish or the Hutterian Brethren are born into them.

The moral values of the members of many contemporary American sects are fundamentally no different that the traditional moral orientations of orthodox Christians (Johnson 1961). Furthermore, some of these sects do not direct their members away from the world but serve as "powerful agent(s) in socializing lower-class groups in the values and usages of our predominantly middle-class society" (Johnson 1957:92). Participation in Holiness sects, for example, has been found to be conducive to upward mobility. Sect affiliation tends to separate those who are upwardly mobile from those underclass people who are resigned to their fate. This is quite a different image of sects than the one usually portrayed in the media.

Sectlike developments within traditional churches raise additional questions about the usefulness of the church/sect typology for understanding contemporary American society. Informal groups within formal religious organizations, such as the Jewish *havurot* (plural of *havurah*) or the charismatic groups within the Catholic church display many sectlike characteristics, even though they meet

---

3. As unbelievable as the idea of an established church in America seems today, nine of the thirteen American colonies did have such an officially recognized church. The Congregational church was "established" in New Hampshire, Massachusetts, and Connecticut, while the Anglican church was the established church in New York, New Jersey, Virginia, Georgia, and the Carolinas. Despite the Bill of Rights, the established church continued in that status in New Hampshire until 1817, in Connecticut until 1818, and in Massachusetts until 1833 (Jameson 1967; Meyer 1930).

under the auspices of a church-type organization. Community service projects and informal study groups are frequently sponsored by churches; not the least reason for sponsoring these is the desire to give participants some of the benefits usually ascribed to sect membership.

The emergence of many non-Christian cults has also weakened the power of the church/sect typology. While many of these cults, especially the more esoteric Oriental cults, share a number of the characteristics generally ascribed to the sect type (such as rejection of the world, a total commitment to the cult, and distinguishing life-styles and conspicuous dress that separate the devotees from non-members), other non-Christian cults do not fit the sect type. The International Society of KRSNA Consciousness (Hare Krishna) is an example of the former, while Scientology is an example of the latter. Furthermore, many cults, including some of those that seek to supplant existing institutional churches, echo traditional American religious values. An anthropologist who studied the Krishna cult for many years reported that devotees are trying to prove that they can live by such traditional values as salvation through good works, spiritual growth through prayer, repentance from sin, and so forth—the very values that also guide the adherents of many Christian sects (Daner 1974). Some suggest therefore that the traditional church sect typology no longer helps them understand the proliferation of cults in contemporary America.

Wilson (1982), however, thought that there was still value to the church sect typology. He suggested that it might be helpful to divide the sect type into two subtypes, as follows:

• The world-affirming or world-enhancing type: sects and cults that seek to improve the skills and competencies of their members so that they may better enjoy the world. Christian Science and Scientology are examples of this type.

• The world-rejecting, world-denying, or world-indifferent type: sects and cults that emphasize salvation from the evils of the world. Efforts are made to separate believers from the ever-present danger of nonbelievers. Some do this by emphasizing particularistic rituals, while others organize separate communes and even separate economic systems. Examples of this type include Pentacostal sects, Jehovah's Witnesses, and the Krsna Consciousness movement.

Social Class and Church Membership

Different religious types may be associated with different social classes. Some have suggested that sect membership is typical of the lower classes, while membership in a church-type organization is characteristic of the upper classes. Max Weber supported this view. According to him, members of the privileged class will be less interested in saving their souls, but will assign to religion "the primary function of legitimizing their own life pattern and situation in the world" (Weber 1963:107). The church type of religion is far better equipped to accomplish this than is the sect type. On the other hand, many members of the lower class view salvation as "an ethic of compensation" for all of the deprivations that they experience in their daily struggle to survive. This function is best met by the sect type (Weber 1963:97). Troeltsch also came to these conclusions. However, there is far from universal agreement with these views. Gilbert (1980) noted that in England as early as the middle of the last century the nonconformist sects were composed largely of members of the middle class. As Queen Victoria's reign lengthened, the English lower classes became increasingly suspicious that the nonconformist sects served to maintain the hegemony of the middle class over the proletariat. This, according to Gilbert, accounts for the early estrangement of the English working class from all organized religion, even from sects.

The thesis that there is a relationship between church/sect and social class found many followers in America. Niebuhr (1929) is credited with writing the classic statement of this proposition. Pope's research of a North Carolina mill town in 1929 provided empirical evidence for the proposition (Pope 1942). Almost thirty years later Morland studied the churches of the mill towns in the Piedmont section of the Carolinas and found a similar class segregation (Morland 1958). Underwood (1957) found the same class segregation in the churches of Paper City, a southern New England industrial city. In each of these studies, the "sect" membership came essentially from the lower class, while the middle and upper classes joined the "churches."

The proposition that socioeconomic status and religiosity are related is reminiscent of the deprivation hypothesis, which suggests that socioeconomic deprivation leads individuals to become more religious. Wimberley (1984) investigated whether such deprivation also led people to place more importance on their religion. Prior research had suggested that religion became more important and more salient as people suffer more deprivation, but Wimberley found that low income (economic deprivation) had no discernable impact on the salience of religion; low status (social deprivation), on the other hand, was positively associated with higher rates of salience of religion.

The relation between socioeconomic status and religiosity probably has become weaker in recent times. As the hippies of the 1960s sought identification and meaning in a variety of different religious groups, class lines became increasingly blurred. Currently, people from all socioeconomic classes are drawn to evangelical sects and esoteric cults. The question of whether this is a temporary phenomenon in response to a specific crisis that faces our society, or a basic societal realignment, needs further study.

Chapter Three

Values and Ideologies in Professional Practice

The differences that a social worker's values and ideology will make in her or his professional practice will be examined in this chapter. Imagine for a moment that a client approached three different social workers and presented to each one the same problem. It is quite possible that each of these three social workers would respond in a different way. One might define the problem as the client's behavior, another might locate the problem in the client's unconscious feelings, and the third might point the finger at society's malfunctions. These practice differences might be grounded in differing value orientations. If asked on what they based their approach, each might cite one or another "professional value." However, it is not always clear whether the value cited is only a rationale for the decision or whether it actually served as a selection-screen for the decision choice.

Social work goals and strategies frequently are selected on the basis of their compatibility with a worker's ideology or values rather than in terms of the demands of the problem or the needs of the client. Rosen and Connaway (1969) have noted that "social workers have tended to choose their methods primarily on the basis of value consistency, disregarding the criteria of method efficacy and purpose-method correspondence." This observation should be viewed in terms of the values of the social work profession. Most social workers have accepted a practice ideology that gives primacy or priority to a client's expressed request, to the client's definition of the problem, and to the client's formulation of the desired goals.

This preference is thought to be consistent with society's belief in democratic values. From this practice ideology flow a number of practice strategies, such as the full involvement of the client in all phases of the intervention process. Yet there is little empirical knowledge to support the efficacy of such practice strategies, just as there is insufficient data to support the practice strategies adopted by most other professions, that the professional practitioner knows better than the client or patient what is needed. Few social workers would endorse the values implicit in Max Weber's statement that "I should think myself a very poor (practitioner) if I did not believe myself to know better than those blockheads what is really good for them" (cited by Michels 1959:230n). But this is precisely the value that governs the behavior of many practitioners in most other professions. Almost all social workers, on the other hand, reject the possibility that their knowledge and their skill may be superior to that of the client because such a view is not compatible with their ideology.

Impact of Values on Practice

All people develop assumptions about themselves and about the world in which they live. These assumptions make it possible to plan actions, to predict the response of others to these actions, and to estimate the consequences and outcomes of these activities. These assumptions are often implicit. They are based on life experiences, which for many persons include their religious experiences. Different people have different life experiences and, therefore, evolve different assumptions. The relationship between these assumptions and an individual's personal value set is reflexive. Values influence the development of a person's assumptions and assumptions, in turn, influence the values that a person adopts.

Values and ideologies are not rarefied abstractions, far removed from daily life. Instead, they have a direct impact on what everyone does every day. Just as people may not realize that they speak in prose, so they are often not aware that they make constant reference to their values and ideologies and use these as criteria for reaching important decisions. Let us examine (on the basis of a specific example) how the assumptions and value sets held by various social workers can lead to different practice decisions. In the following vignette I present a case illustration that many social workers will recognize as familiar.

Case 3.1: Jill Is Pregnant

Jill, a fourteen-year-old seventh grader, is eight weeks pregnant. She was sent to the school social worker by the school nurse. Before sending the student, the nurse asked the social worker to make all the necessary arrangements for an abortion.

Jill came for her appointment on time. The worker's first impressions were that Jill gave the appearance of an "average" fourteen-year-old. She was quite verbal and smiled frequently. She had no hesitation in discussing the fact that she had been sexually active for a long time and that she was now pregnant. But she refused to reveal the name of the child's father. She was sure that she did not want an abortion. She wanted to have the baby, even if this might result in her having to drop out of school.

Different social workers will follow different strategies with Jill.[1] Some will respect Jill's request to continue her pregnancy. They will base their decision on the professional value of client self-determination, that is, the right of every client to decide his or her own fate. Even though this client is only fourteen years old, she has a right to decide what she wants to do about her situation. Other social workers will act differently, basing their decision on a worker's ethical obligation to protect the best interests of both the present client and the fetus she is carrying. They will proceed to arrange for an abortion, arguing that Jill is not sufficiently mature to make such an irreversible decision.

If we really want to understand a social worker's decision in this case, (no matter what that decision was), we must analyze that worker's values concerning human life, abortion, and education. When we know what these are, we will be in a better position to understand the practice decision taken. In Jill's case, as in so many other practice situations, goals and strategies are often selected on the

1. All of the vignettes and cases in this volume are purposefully abridged in order to focus attention on the particular aspect of the case discussed. In Jill's case, for example, no caseworker would make a decision until there was a more thorough discussion with Jill about her wishes and desires. Both Jill and the worker need much more insight into the various parts of the problem than appears from the all too brief exemplar here. Nevertheless, decisions must be made, even after the social worker understands more fully what Jill is saying—whether to let Jill "decide," whether and how to intervene, or whatever other decision seems indicated.

basis of their compatibility with the worker's ideology and values. What is "best for the client" depends in no small measure on the worker's values. The social worker who believes that the fetus is already alive will hesitate to assist in arranging an abortion, while a colleague who is convinced that life starts only after birth will have few qualms about such a strategy. Kuhn noted that the followers of different ideologies "practice their trade in different worlds [and] see different things when they look from the same point in the same direction" (1970:149).

Additional support for the proposition that values and ideologies provide the major base for social work decisions has come from the consistent rejection by most social workers of research findings that suggest that low levels of worker activity are not always helpful when working with lower-class clients. With many of these persons a more aggressive worker style might be indicated. Such findings are usually ignored because they seem to go against the professional ideology that suggests that workers should be as inactive as possible in order to maximize client participation (Kadushin 1972; Mullen 1969). Social workers are not the only professionals whose practice is influenced by ideology. This is a common phenomenon, encountered in almost every profession. Even in medicine, reputedly the most scientific of all professions, the treatment of choice is often determined as much by ideology as by knowledge. An historical example was the use of female circumcision by nineteenth-century physicians as the treatment of choice for many mental and physical illnesses that women of that day were believed to suffer (Barker-Benfield 1976). Today, shock therapy and other punitive treatment modalities reflect a commitment to moral values that the official medical profession has rejected, but which persist and still guide, perhaps unconsciously, some physicians (Menninger 1973).

Some have suggested that values play a more important part in social work practice decisions than is true for many other contemporary professions. One observer noted that "no other profession, with the exception perhaps of philosophy, concerns itself as deeply with the matter of values as does the profession of social work" (Brown 1968). Pumphrey described social work as "a heavily value-laden profession" and wrote that this emphasis on values is especially important "because social work touches so many individual and social facets of life [that] it is easy for a worker to lose his feeling for the ultimate purpose of his work" (1959:12). Others have explained the relatively greater commitment of social workers to values by noting the insufficiency of relevant empirical knowledge (Rees 1978). Lack of knowledge makes for uncertainty. Situations of uncertainty are common in social work practice. In uncertain situations social workers tend to place a greater reliance on values because these give an appearance of certainty (Light 1979). Still others have suggested that the priority given to the value base is inherent and essential to social work practice. Thus, Vigilante noted that "social workers have religiously clung to values over the seventy years of the development of the profession. . . . We seem to cling to them intuitively, out of faith, as a symbol of humanitarianism" (1974:114).

Defining Values and Ideologies

In the previous pages I freely used such terms as value, value orientation, preference, ideology, and belief, as if they meant more or less the same thing. But do they really have the same or similar meanings? It is obvious that in the literature these terms have no fixed definition so that one author's values might be discussed by another writer under the heading of "beliefs." Many, like Lee, "speak of value but [are] not prepared to define it" (1953:335). And yet the reader is entitled to know how these terms are defined here.

Aschenbrenner (1971) analyzed almost three thousand different usages of the concept "value." A popular dictionary offers no less than seventeen definitions of the term, and Timms (1983) noted that a review of reports and publications from a wide variety of fields found no less than one hundred different definitions for it. An informal survey of social work books and journals suggests that almost as many definitions have been used by social work authors.

Maslow may have described the situation accurately when he observed that values are like a big container that holds all sorts of miscellaneous and vague things (1962:158). Many philosophers have used the term "value" as if it meant the same as "interest," but Dewey (1922) used the term in a more precise way by noting that a value must include some element of appraisal or preference. Social scientists generally have followed Dewey's usage by indicating that values are meant to serve as guides or criteria for selecting appropriate behaviors. Bartlett used "value" to refer to what is regarded as good or desirable (1970:63).

Williams identified values as "those conceptions of desirable states of affairs that are utilized in selective conduct as criteria for preference or choice or as justification for proposed or actual behavior" (1967:23). Guy emphasized the role of values as "a template for decision making" (1985:22). Kluckhohn added that "a value is not just a preference but it is a preference which is felt and/or considered to be justified" (1951:306). Similarly, I will use the term "value" as a criterion for decision making, giving guidance for selecting appropriate behaviors.

The way "value" is used today is of relatively recent origin. The current usage entered our vocabulary only in the nineteenth century. But the term was already used in the Bible in its economic meaning (see, for example, Leviticus 27:3). Throughout the centuries "value" was synonymous with "worth." It was this definition that led Adam Smith to talk about value-in-use. Philosophers began to use the term only in the middle of the last century in place of what they had previously called "the good." Before the end of the nineteenth century this newer definition was already in wide use in daily English speech.

Values differ from one another along four dimensions: generality, intensity, persistence, and content.

GENERALITY

Ultimate values deal with generalized conceptions of the world, of a person's place in it, and of a person's relations to God and/or to fellow human beings. *Instrumental values* translate an ultimate value into operational terms. For example, the ultimate value of "respect for the dignity of each individual" finds expression in such instrumental values as "confidentiality." The relation between ultimate and instrumental values is not always clear (Pumphrey 1959:41). Greater clarity in this dimension would be especially helpful for social workers because their profession assigns such a high priority to values. However, Bloom advocated that the helping professions limit themselves to instrumental values only and not be concerned with ultimate values. Practitioners should focus on what values look like as they are expressed in action rather than engage in philosophical contemplations about the relations between ultimate and instrumental values (Bloom 1975:138).

INTENSITY

Values differ in the intensity with which they are held. It is not sufficient to examine the values that a person holds without at the same time taking into consideration the intensity with which they are held (Mobley and Locke 1970). The most intensely held values are sometimes called *beliefs*. Intensely held values are usually anchored in both an intellectual and an emotional affirmation of the value's rightness. When a value is not so moored, it may receive only superficial adherence without much conviction and with little intensity. Though most people subscribe to the value of marital faithfulness, the different levels of intensity with which this value is held may explain varying behavior patterns.

PERSISTENCE

Values generally are enduring, though some are more enduring than others. Generally, ultimate values and those most intensely held are most enduring. But even among instrumental values, some are more enduring than others (McCormick 1975).

CONTENT

Social values refer to preferable relations between an individual and other persons, while *spiritual values* deal with the relations between a person and God and the universe, and to ideas about the purpose and meaning of life.

The ancient Greeks made value decisions solely on the basis of rational considerations. They were not fully aware of the distinction between values and knowledge. Consequently they held that a person could hope to come into possession of "the good" only by way of reason. The dichotomy between value and knowledge first appeared in the early days of the evolution of Christian thought when for some the ethical came to be more important than the rational. But other Christian philosophers and theologians, including Thomas Aquinas and Duns Scotius, both neo-Aristoteleans, attempted to develop an integrated ethical and knowledge base for human behavior. In modern times, when the Kantian categorical imperative became replaced by an egoistic relativism, this ethical base has become increasingly diluted (Dewey 1929:51–52). According to one contemporary approach, almost everything that people want can be considered a value — health, honesty, freedom, as well as money, drugs, fame, and even cockfighting (Barry 1973). In this and similar philosophical systems, people no longer seek "the good" because whatever it is that people want is thereby declared a value.

The term *ideology* has also been used in a number of different ways. Though sometimes this term has negative connotations, it is used here to represent the system of beliefs and values that give expression to a group's distinctive ideas and ideals. Thus Parsons defined ideology as a "system of beliefs held in common by members of a collectivity" (1951:349). Ideology involves some level of commitment as an aspect of group membership. This use of ideology is similar to the way Kuhn used the term "paradigm" as referring to "the entire constellation of beliefs, values, techniques and so on shared by the members of a given community" (1970:175). The purpose of an ideology is to minimize individual behavior differences by identifying group goals and group-preferred techniques in order that individual members will engage in behaviors that will contribute toward the common goal. A professional ideology shapes a profession's public identity. Furthermore, a professional ideology "may motivate and support the use of a profession's value system and practice principles" (Siporin 1975:75). In this way the professional ideology serves as a guideline for purposeful professional activity.

Ideology may give meaning to otherwise incomprehensible social situations by letting people reinterpret the ambiguous into something familiar. Ideology permits practitioners to make sense out of what they are doing, particularly when they find themselves in uncertain situations. Thus, ideology is particularly important in practice areas where knowledge is still incomplete. This principle holds not only for social work, but for all fields of practice and knowledge, even the physical sciences, because no field has acquired all of the knowledge that its practitioners need (Kuhn 1970; Rees 1978; Yelloly 1980).

Value and Knowledge in the Social Work Practice Base

Social work practice is based on three interacting elements: values, knowledge, and skills. However, the relationship between these three elements, and particularly between knowledge and values, is problematic. Some speak of a knowledge/value dilemma. Though social work practice theory indicates that there is a reciprocal relationship between values and knowledge, on the one hand, and between knowledge and skills, on the other, the realization of this promise has been disappointing (Gordon 1965a). The problematic nature of this relationship may be due to social work's reliance on social science theory. While some social workers have argued for an interpenetration of knowledge and values, most have accepted the traditional social science demand which requires a strict separation between these two elements. This demand is presented most forcefully by those social workers who follow the positivist tradition, which posits that only empirical data that are value neutral can lead to knowledge development.

But the essentiality of value-free knowledge is denied by many who hold that knowledge about human beings and about the human situation can never be value neutral. They point out that the attempt to avoid values has resulted at times in research studies that were methodologically exact and used all of the appropriate statistics, but were nevertheless meaningless because they did not address real concerns. Thus, Lerner and Laswell once observed that "a science of nothing may be rigorous but is not capable of explaining anything of importance" (1951:28). Habermas (1971) wrote that a value-free social science is both an unnecessary and an incoherent scientific ideal. He argued that a social science that says anything significant about social life cannot be value neutral.

Even though many think that values cannot and should not be separated from knowledge in developing the social work practice base, they do not always indicate clearly the specific relationship between these two elements. But those who follow the radical approach *have* identified this relationship; they maintain that knowledge and values are inseparably welded together. Values direct the search for knowledge since values establish the conceptual framework for interpretation, which screens evidence. Changes in knowledge, in turn, promote value changes (Jones 1975). Others have suggested that the relationship between knowledge and values is reflexive. When the knowledge available is insufficient for the task on hand, social workers will depend more heavily on values to guide their practice choices. As social work knowledge becomes more widely available, values will occupy a less prominent role in professional decision making. This reflexive relationship most probably holds not only for social work but for all professional fields.

We must remember, however, that "knowledge" is socially defined. A witch doctor may by our standards have very little "scientific" knowledge, but in his own society he is believed to possess a great deal of important knowledge (Goode 1969:282). In other words, values determine to a significant degree what constitutes knowledge! A society that has endorsed secular values will disparage religious knowledge because this type of knowledge cannot be verified by the culturally accepted knowledge criteria. But this same knowledge will meet with approval in a society that has a greater commitment to religious values. This suggests that there is, in fact, a very close relationship between values and knowledge. It was this thought that led Kuhn (1970) to observe that the type of knowledge developed in any one society at any given time depends very much on the predominating societal values.

Ideology and values are far from a second-best substitute for knowledge. They are important for every profession, but in the practice base of social work they are important elements in their own right. Guzzetta warned social workers that if the quest for scientific knowledge and empirical findings ever led to a "neglect of the axiological considerations, we shall lose not only the justification for continuing to seek professional identity, but also our entire historical heritage" (1966:43). Gordon also taught that professional values constitute "the major substance of social work" (1965b:20). Though values and ideology may be emphasized today because knowledge is still incomplete, this emphasis will presumably continue even when the profession has a more fully developed body of knowledge.

Those bewailing the inadequacy of social work knowledge base their claim on the findings of a relatively large number of empirical research studies which documented the lack of consensus between what social workers do and what they say they know (Bartlett 1970;

Compton and Galaway 1979; Curnock and Hardiker 1979; Hardiker and Barker 1981; Yelloly 1980; and many others). But one could argue that not using knowledge (or better, that a social worker's inability to report to the researcher the theoretical knowledge on which a particular practice decision was based) is not necessarily proof that this knowledge does not exist. The knowledge that exists may not be available in usable form; knowledge dissemination may be faulty; or there may be other reasons why social workers do not use the knowledge that is available. Alternately, the so-called knowledge/practice gap may represent something quite different than a scarcity of knowledge. It may well be that social workers know a great deal more than what they are able to recall or report verbally. Their practice gives evidence of the mastery of a relatively large body of knowledge. More recent studies provide evidence that social workers do deliver effective service. These studies strongly suggest that practice decisions are the result of informed choices, based on some type of knowledge (Reid and Hanrahan 1982; Thomlison 1984).

Is There a Unitary Professional Ideology?

This emphasis on the value base gives urgency to the question whether the social work profession has a unitary ideology. Most writers assume that there is a common professional ideology and one professional value set that all social workers do (or should) accept. Bisno (1952) argued that social work had a unitary philosophical base. McLeod and Meyer (1967) found in an empirical study that the values of professional social workers tended to cluster and to differ from the values of practitioners of other professions. Keith-Lucas (1971) described this ideology as *humanistic, positivistic,* and *utopian.*

At one time, not too many years ago, there may have been a high degree of value homogeneity among social workers. The wide acceptance of a unitary professional ideology led to repeated demands that all social workers accept it. Pumphrey stated that "it seems axiomatic" that new recruits to social work must accept the common professional values before they can be considered bona fide professionals (1959:12). Nichols wrote that "those who cannot adhere to the profession's consensual values cannot join" (1979). And Levy (1976a), who chaired the NASW committee that formulated the professional code of ethics, argued that whenever there is a conflict between professional values and personal values, a social worker must give priority to the former.

The proposition that there is a unitary social work ideology is in line with the widely accepted theorem in the sociology of professions: that the members of any one profession share in common more values than they share with members of other professions. However, a number of authors and researchers have begun to question this theorem. Years ago Bucher and Strauss (1961) questioned the view that each profession is a relatively homogeneous community whose members share an identify, values, and preferences. Box and Cotgrove (1966) found within any one profession a number of different value sets; they concluded that these differences reflected differences in the work settings in which professionals practiced. According to these authors, the work setting rather than the professional affiliation makes for identity. Guy (1985) examined the values and preferences of members of various professions, including social workers, who were employed in different mental hospitals. She concluded:

Members of a discipline are not birds of a feather who flock together, holding the same value schemata. Members of one profession often have more in common with members of a different profession than with the members of their own. This research shows that the amount of agreement within a profession is organization specific. While social workers at Alpha [Mental Hospital] were of one mind, at Omega [Mental Hospital] they were markedly more diverse. (Guy 1985:173)

In other words, the proposition of professional value consensus or homogeneity needs to be revised or, at least, needs further empirical testing. In line with this approach, Timms (1983) rejected the idea that there is one set of social work values to which all social workers agree. He pointed out (as I did earlier in this chapter) that in identical situations different social workers will arrive at different practice decisions. Even Levy, who demanded that professionals give priority to professional values when these are in conflict with personal values, admitted that the profession's ideology is still in a "state of emergence" (1976b:115).

It is far from clear whether the current estimate of value multiplicity represents a basic change from the earlier representation of value homogeneity. There may not be any real disagreement between those who hold that there is one unitary professional ideology and those who reject this notion. Adherents of both views probably agree that at the highest level of generality there is a common ideology, but that this unanimity fades away as the ideology is brought down to a more immediate and practical action level. There is a wide consensus about basic professional value orientations, as expressed in the *NASW Code of Ethics* (which will be discussed below). While there may be agreement on these ultimate values, there are divergent approaches to the relevant instrumental values for professional decision making. Everyone agrees that "maintenance of life" is a high-priority professional value, but there is disagreement about the definition of "life" on the action level. Is a fetus "alive"? After how many weeks? What about a person whose brain has ceased to function but whose heart still shows a trace of activity? (For a discussion of the implications of recent medical advances on social work practice, see Abramson and Black 1985). Guy also made reference to the two-level approach to professional values; she noted that the values that are taught in professional schools are very broad in nature and often not relevant to the practitioner's day-to-day concerns. Such values do "not contribute to decision making at the workplace where the profession is practiced" (1985:87).

Values and Behavior

Even though ideologies and values are meant to serve as guides for selecting desirable behaviors, they do not always act as such. A person's behavior is not always consistent with his or her professed values. For example, client participation in decision making is highly valued by almost all social workers, yet many do not always make sufficient effort to involve clients fully. One reason for the lack of congruence between values and behaviors may be that values are usually stated at a very high level of generality while behaviors are very specific. Another reason for this lack of congruence may be the gap between the professed (public) and the real (personal) values that a person holds.

There is broad agreement about most ultimate values, such as cooperation and success, but these are not sufficiently specific to help identify appropriate behavior patterns. The more specific a value, the more useful it will be as a behavioral guide. But the more specific a value, the smaller the chance that it will receive wide acceptance. For example, almost everyone agrees that "family life" is a highly desired value, that is, as long as that value is not defined in more specific operational terms. But this generalized value does not help an adult son who has to make a difficult decision about how to care for his paralyzed, senile father without increasing the tension that already exists between his present wife and his children from a previous marriage. Nor will this generalized value help the son's social worker discover specific action referents that may offer guidance for this situation.

A number of attempts have been made to state the basic general value orientation of social work. The revised *Curriculm Policy Statement* of the Council on Social Work Education (1982) summarized the core values of the social work profession in the following way:

1. Social workers' professional relationships are built on their regard for individual worth and human dignity and are furthered by mutual participation, acceptance, confidentiality, honesty, and responsible handling of conflict.

2. Social workers respect people's right to choose, to contract for services, and to participate in the helping process.

3. Social workers contribute to making social institutions more humane and responsive to human needs.

4. Social workers demonstrate respect for and acceptance of the unique characteristics of diverse populations.

5. Social workers are responsible for their own ethical conduct, for the quality of their practice, and for maintaining continuous growth in the knowledge and skills of their profession.

The problem with lists of basic professional values, such as the one just presented, is that as long as they remain generalized and nonspecific, they do not offer sufficient behavioral guidance. Social workers are likely to engage in a variety of different, at times even contradictory, activities, while claiming to support the same generalized professional value. This situation let Perlman to conclude that "a value has small worth, except as it is moved, or is moveable, from believing into doing, from verbal affirmation into action" (1976:381).

When social work professional values are presented at a high level of generality it is entirely possible for different social workers to engage in very different activities, while justifying their choices by citing the identical value. For example, in a study of the way social workers operationalize the value of self-determination, Kossal and Kane (1980) found "a great variability in the way practitioners interpret and apply the concept . . . in specific situations." As long as the professional ideology is expressed at such a generalized level, an individual social worker's personal beliefs, especially religious beliefs, may have a stronger impact on practice choices than the professional ideology (Faver 1985).

There are occasions when social workers with different value profiles seem to make identical practice decisions. In a preliminary study both religious and secular social workers were found who indicated support for Jill's request (case 3.1) not to abort. The former cited religious values that prohibit abortions, while the latter based the identical practice decision on their support of the social work value of self-determination. This suggests that the relation between values and practice is far from simple (Baum et al. 1987).

Our discussion has followed the generally accepted view that values and attitudes determine or influence behavioral choices. However, some attitude theorists have suggested another sequence and have provided experimental evidence that it is actually behavior that influences the choice of attitudes and values (Bem 1970; Festinger 1957). The influence of social factors in the selection of values is emphasized by others; acording to this view, persons will tend to select beliefs and values that are in consonance with their social experiences (White 1970). After reviewing all the available evidence, Acock and Fuller (1984) suggested a reciprocal model where values influence behavioral choices and behaviors influence value choices. In line with this view is Moberg's (1982) observation that the greater the salience of one's religious experiences, the more likely that religious values and attitudes will influence one's behavior.

I noted earlier that values have a specific impact on knowledge, despite the positivist predilection for separating these two elements.

Some religious values have had a specific impact on the development of social work knowledge. For example, much of our knowledge about relationships was initially derived from the works of existentialist theologians, such as Buber, Tillich, and Maritain. Yet it would be inaccurate to claim that religious values have had a major impact on contemporary social work knowledge. Though the pioneer social workers were undoubtedly influenced by religious values, even when they rejected formal religious practices, most current professional knowledge is derived from other than religious sources.

The Problem of Uncertainty

There is one other aspect of the knowledge/value dilemma that we need to discuss here briefly because it has implications for the analysis of the impact of religious thought on social work practice. Uncertainty is a characteristic endemic to social work practice. A social worker is almost always uncertain about the specific cause of a client's problem; nor can the outcome of a specific intervention strategy usually be predicted with any great accuracy. Dewey noted that "the distinctive characteristic of practical activity . . . is the uncertainty which attends to it" (1929:6). Uncertainty creates discomfort. The natural response is an attempt to reduce this discomfort.

Two discomfort reduction strategies are commonly utilized by social workers: scientific social work principles and methods are adopted because it is believed that science, which is based on certainty, will diminish uncertainty; and religious values are utilized since these are believed to deal with permanent truths. In the past, most social workers chose the first option, but in recent years many have discovered that science is not as certain as they had been led to believe. One prominent medical researcher recently wrote, "The greatest of all accomplishments of 20th century science has been the discovery of human ignorance" (Thomas 1981). Much earlier Heisenberg destroyed forever the illusion that the exact sciences were based entirely on empirically derived facts and that these could provide certainty in an uncertain world. His "principle of indeterminacy" underlined the uncertainty that prevails everywhere, even in modern science (Heisenberg 1958).

Yet the need to find certainty remains a basic human require-ment. As social workers became aware of the uncertainties of the "exact" sciences, an increasing number began to turn to the second option of reducing uncertainty. The need to find certainty has led some to hold on to an idea even when demonstrably it is no longer adequate. Still others have rushed to adopt new ideas before these have been sufficiently tested, even when they seem no more adequate for reducing uncertainty than those that they replaced. Social workers, both those committed to religious values and those committed to other values, must learn to cope with and make creative use of uncertainty because the world is full of it. Professional social work practice will always be equivocal. This is the nature of the problems with which we deal.

Religious and Secular Values

At one time, before the profession of social work was "born," almost everyone engaged in charitable work. The values associated with char-ity were rooted deeply in religion. In every generation preachers urged the faithful to engage in philanthropic and charitable work as an expres-sion of their religious faith. In the eighteenth century Cotton Mather preached that the performance of good deeds is an obligation to God and not a mere means to salvation; he therefore urged that all men and women engage in "a perpetual endeavor to do good in the world" (1966). Early in the ninteenth century, popular revivalists like Charles Grandison Finney demanded from new converts that they engage in charitable works and social action immediately after and as part of their being born again (McCarthy 1982). But times have changed.

Most contemporary authors agree that nowadays social work values are based on secular, humanist values. No doubt, there are individual social workers who sometimes (or always) utilize religious values in their practice, but these values are rarely mentioned in the professional literature. Most professional social workers feel that a religious value orientation does not have any importance in contem-porary social work practice. Many think that those who do utilize religious values are out of the mainstream of social work practice.

Whether this is really so needs empirical study. The contrary is entirely possible. A religious value orientation may be more in line with the clients' value orientation, while a secular, humanist value orientation may be out of touch with the culture in which social work is practiced.

Some have suggested that it makes little difference whether a social worker's personal values are secular or religious since it is a cardinal professional principle that every social worker attempt to neutralize his or her own values when serving clients. It is, of course, crucial to make every effort not to impose one's own values on a client. Nevertheless, many have felt that one's personal values do make a difference. Take the situation facing Carl (case 3.2). No social worker who faces this situation can avoid the impact of his or her own personal values on the questions raised by Carl.

Case 3.2: Carl Is Gay

Carl is 17 years old. He approached a social worker in the community center to discuss his problem. Over the past two years he has been involved in several homosexual relationships. He is ambivalent about these. On the one hand, he obtained a great deal of satisfaction from them. On the other hand, he feels guilty about them, and wants some advice.

It was found that different social workers responded in different ways to Carl's plea for help. There were those who defined Carl's problem as his "guilt" and essentially tried to help him to resolve these guilt feelings. Other social workers defined Carl's homosexual relations as the problem and tried to help him understand this so that he might consider changing this behavior. When asked to account for the strategy or goal they had selected, both groups of social workers cited one or another professional value to justify their approach. But it is reaonable to suspect that in situations such as these (where it is far from clear which professional value is relevant), the worker's personal beliefs, including religious beliefs, will give guidance to practice decisions (McMinn 1984).

The importance of personal values, especially religious values, in professional decision making was also supported by the earlier study of McLeod and Meyer (1967). In the Social Work Value Test, developed especially for this study, high scores represented the values that were assumed to correspond to the "dominant" professional social work value position, while low scores indicated the opposite of non-social work values. For seven out of ten value dimensions tested, there was a significant statistical relation between the worker's religious background and the value score. Religiously identified Protestant and Catholic social workers achieved low scores, while those without any religious commitment tended to achieve high scores. Clearly secularist nonbelievers reported different values than affiliated Christians. Religious belief or nonbelief does seem to have an impact on professional practice positions.

However, I have not been able to find empirical support for the existence of a wide gap between believers and nonbelievers. While there is a cluster of values and behaviors associated with each group, there is a good deal of crossing over or value blurring amoung individuals identified with each group. Some secular social workers, in some situations, give what appear to be religious value responses, just as some religious social workers, in some situations, give secular value responses. This may be due in part to the fact that the social work value system, though it is today primarily humanistic and positivistic, has strong religious trends (Siporin 1975:69). This observation is of some importance because "much of therapy actually involves helping people to choose their ways of life in the light of ethical principles so as to do good and to act rightly and justly" (Siporin 1985b:24). Maslow made a similar observation; "If behavioral scientists are to solve human problems, the question of right and wrong behavior is essential. It is the very essence of behavioral science" (cited by Bergin 1982).

Not everyone will agree with the statement that it is one of the social worker's functions to help clients choose between right and wrong behaviors on the basis of ethical principles. This approach is questioned for various reasons. The relativists reject the notion that there is one right or correct way of behavior that applies to all people in all situations. Because of this they wonder what special insight gives social workers the authority to decide what is right or wrong. The religionists may agree with Siporin's formulation but wonder whether most social workers are really equipped to render help based on ethical principles. Their doubts are based on their understanding that the major professional social work ideology is humanistic and positivistic and does not make reference to religious values, and it is these religious values that they consider particularly relevant for questions of right and wrong.

TABLE 3.1. Religious Values Contrasted with Secular Values

Religious Values	Secular Values
1. God is supreme.	1. The individual is supreme.
2. Obedience of God's will.	2. Autonomy and rejection of external authority.
3. Personal identity is eternal.	3. Personal identity is transitory.
4. Self-worth depends on one's relationship with God.	4. Self-worth depends on one's relationship with others.
5. Absolute values, universal ethics, categorical imperatives.	5. Relative values, situational ethics, flexible morality.
6. Love, service, and sacrifice are central to personal growth.	6. Self-actualization and self-fulfillment are central to personal growth.
7. Commitment to marriage, fidelity, procreation, and family life.	7. Emphasis on self-gratification and/or recreational sex within or outside of marriage.
8. Personal responsibility for one's actions and for any harmful effects; acceptance of guilt and contrition as an opportunity for change.	8. A person is not necessarily responsible for one's own or for another's problems; guilt should be minimized before it causes emotional damage.

Source: adapted from Bergin 1980 and 1982

In the past little attention was paid to the difference between religious and secular values and their respective impact on social work practice. Those authors who have been concerned with the problem of the value-practice relation usually utilized a unitary professional value set, developed at a very high level of generalization so that it could apply to all social workers, both secular and religious (for example, Howard 1969). But it may be preferable to develop a set of values at a somewhat lower level of generality, a level that will permit the formulation of specfic religious and secular values. This, in turn, may permit a more accurate investigation of the impact of religious values on social work practice. Bergin (1980, 1982) identified such specific value sets when he explored the difference that religious and secular values made for psychologists. In table 3.1 I utilized his ideas in order to develop separate sets of secular and religious values that I believe are relevant for social work practice.

Admittedly, the "religious values" identified here are biased toward traditional Western religious values, while the "secular values" are those that are identified with the Western humanistic, positivist tradition. Such a dichotomous value presentation does not do full justice to liberal humanist religious thought and virtually ignores the value sets of contemporary radical religious theologians, such as Bonhoeffer, Hromadka, and Teilhard de Chardin. It also fails to take into consideration non-Western values, both religious and secular (if such a dichotomy is relevant to Eastern philosophy). Some non-Western values parallel Western values, but others depart widely from them (Gunsalus 1969). As presented here, the two sides of each value pair are mutually exclusive. But it may be more useful to convert each pair into a value dimension with a large number of intermediate points along the full value range. In this case, the values identified in table 3.1 will represent the two polar positions.

The role of religious values in therapy has been discussed more frequently by psychologists than by social workers (Bergin 1980; Ellis 1980; Walls 1980). McMinn has noted that many of these discussions have dealt with global issues rather than with more specific values and their application to specific practice situations. He has suggested that "the practical relevance of religious values in psychotherapy exists primarily at the level of client-therapist matching, and not at the universal level" (1984). However, it seems that McMinn himself failed to explore the more general problem of how specific religious values impact on practice. I will attempt to do this here for social work practice. Only in the next chapter shall I take up the question of client-worker matching.

The Impact of Specific Values on Practice

I shall limit my examination of the impact of values on practice to a small number of specific values. These values were selected on a random basis. Other specific values could have served equally well as exemplars. The values that I shall examine are individualism (derived from value 1 in table 3.1), self-actualization (value 6), and control of fate (value 8).

INDIVIDUALISM
This secular value is deeply ingrained in the American culture (Slater 1970). American social work, a product of that culture, has given practice application to this value in a number of ways. Yet many

social work authors have questioned the uncritical acceptance of this value by practitioners. Thus, Glick (1977) wrote critically about the "excessive emphasis on individualism" in American society and in social work practice. I noted earlier that this emphasis on individualism has placed a premium on rugged self-reliance, a character trait that perhaps was appropriate for a developing and expanding frontier society but is less functional in contemporary urban life. Many Americans have become incapable of committing themselves to basic social institutions, such as marriage, family, religion, and politics because of the emphasis on individualism. This "radical individualism" may have grown cancerous and may be threatening the survival of freedom itself, according to sociologist Robert Bellah (1985:154–55). The unqualified acceptance of radical individualism by social workers may interfere with their ability to help those who suffer from this "cancer."

When the individual is supreme, it is logical to accept his or her definition of what is good and desirable. On the other hand, when God is supreme, the divine definition of what is good and desirable will provide guidance for human activities. How this definition of what is good becomes known to believers is a critical question, but one that is outside the scope of this volume. I shall only note here that fundamentalists find this definition in the revealed word of God, while humanists claim that there must be antecedent knowledge of what is good before it can be attributed to God (Cooney 1985).

Once upon a time, people wanted to do what was good. Now each individual determines what is good. The order of things has been reversed. Instead of wanting to do what is good, whatever a person does or wants is now defined as good. One can hardly argue that this approach to ethics is entirely new. Spinoza taught three hundred years ago that "we do not desire something because it is good; it is good because we desire it" (1955: Prop. 9, part 3). However, there is a crucial difference here: in his day Spinoza was almost alone, while in the contemporary world this philosophy represents the prevalent view.

Social work's identification of the client's decision as *the* crucial element in the action plan is grounded in the secular value of individualism. There is no question that as long as a client's desire does not seem to harm anyone else, his or her desire should receive high priority consideration. But the fact that everything one person does affects others is often overlooked because of the emphasis placed on this value. If Carl (case 3.2) opts for continued homosexual relations, that is his desire and his wish. This decision should be fully supported by the social worker, no matter how it may affect others (his parents, his peers, his community, etc.). Carl alone has the right to decide how he wants to live.

However, it would be an oversimplification to claim that individualism is only a secular value and to define the relevant religious value as the opposite. Accepting the centrality of God does not necessarily conflict with giving importance to the individual. Humanistic and liberal theologians certainly do not see any conflict. Nineteenth-century Christian revivalists also placed great emphasis on the individual. The most radical expression of this was the adoption of the doctrines of Arminianism, which values personal religious experiences and accepts the authority of the individual above that of church teachings and certified doctrine (Sweet 1944). When Christian fundamentalist churches reject hierarchical authority they also derive this teaching from the individualistic value position, yet they see no conflict between this stance and their belief in the supremacy of God, since they unhesitatingly give priority to the latter. Religionists do not disvalue individualism, yet they do not make it a supervalue.

At times, social workers who accept secular values will make different practice decisions than will their colleagues who follow religious values. A social worker whose practice decisions are guided by religious values will try to help Carl reestablish his value priorities. Since God, rather than the individual, is supreme, this social worker will attempt to make it easier for Carl to follow the Commandments, which proscribe homosexual relations. The focus will be on attempting to introduce behavioral changes. Note that value dimensions 2, 7, and 8 of table 3.1 are also relevant in this practice situation. The secular social worker, on the other hand, may in the first instance not consider any behavioral changes, but will address attention to the problem of relieving Carl's guilt feelings.

A social worker need not be religious, however, to counsel Carl to abandon homosexual relations in order to resolve his guilt feelings. Some may indicate that they are agnostic or atheist, but their value orientation, at least in this area, is impacted by values drawn from religious sources. There is, of course, no need for them to consciously identify the sources of their values. Similarly, there are social workers who attend church regularly and who may follow religious obligations, but whose practice decisions are based on the secular values associated with the professional ideology. Some of these social workers will in this case focus on relieving Carl's guilt feelings without introducing any behavioral change objectives.

The so-called "value-free" argument is not really relevant here. Neither does the social work value of avoiding judgments impact directly on this situation. I will discuss these issues at length in the next chapter. Suffice it to say that in working with Carl, as in most cases, a social worker inevitably expresses a value, no matter what he or she does. Helping Carl to abandon his homosexual behavior expresses a value judgment just as does assuring him that gay relations are acceptable in our society. While nonjudgmentalism (which refers to the way a social worker uses values) is desirable, avoiding values in social work practice is not possible.

SELF-ACTUALIZATION

The accepted social work ideology holds that a person's well-being and freedom are of supreme importance. It is a violation of the professional code of ethics to interfere with these. Self-actualization and self-expression, self-determination and autonomy are only a few of the practice modes based on this value position. A social worker who is guided by secular values may assess Carl's problem in the following way: Carl admits to obtaining a great deal of satisfaction from the homosexual relationship. However, irrational guilt feelings prevent him from maximizing the benefits that he could derive from this experience. Something keeps Carl from self-actualization. A social worker's task is to help Carl to overcome this barrier. Once Carl understands the reasons for his fears and gains sufficient insight to realize that there is no rational basis for them, he may overcome his guilt feelings and benefit from whatever type of relationship he ultimately wishes to engage in.

The corresponding religious values stress the categorical imperative to obey God's will and the desirability of personal growth through love, service, and sacrifice. In every situation where God's will is known, the preferred course of action is to implement this value position. Most religious codes proscribe homosexual behavior. For those who accept the validity of these religious edicts, the preferred social intervention would focus on helping Carl to achieve a change in his behavior. At the same time, most religious social workers recognize that there is often a gap between valued behavior and actual behavior. They differ from secular colleagues in that they would not "sanctify" what they consider deviant behavior. A religious social worker would not condemn Carl if he chose to continue the gay relationship, but he or she would not encourage him to continue this experience or tell him that it did not make any difference whether a person engaged in homosexual or heterosexual behavior.

CONTROL OF ONE'S FATE

Inherent in the accepted social work ideology is the value of individual and social responsibility. The ability to control one's fate and to change it is a key value which differentiates modern secular, scientific values from those of the medieval world of magic and superstition. It is also a key element of the contemporary social work ideology. An outright rejection of this value would counterindicate any possibility for social work intervention.

At the same time there is today a widespread feeling that human beings are no longer completely in control of their fate. Even though (or perhaps because) science and technology are becoming ever more powerful, "men experience themselves as less potent, less in control of their destiny" (Gouldner 1973:76). This feeling leads to apathy, one of the more detrimental consequences of life in today's world. The task of the social worker is to do something about preventing or reversing this apathy. Social caseworkers approach the pathological aspects of the condition clinically, while community social workers and social group workers attempt to work with community and other groups in order to arrest and counter this destructive phenomenon.

The secular belief that a person is (or can be) in control of his or her fate seems to run counter to the belief that God is supreme and controls every person's fate. If it is God's will that a certain situation exists, then there is nothing that can or should be done about it. Human and social problems may reflect God's will to punish people for their sinful behavior. Mortals should not attempt to make any changes that would lighten this punishment. An appeal to God by prayer, or a determined effort to correct the sinful behavior, are the only permissible human activities. These will, at least in the long run, be more effective than any planned social "intervention." According to this ideology, abortion is not a valid option even for Jill (Case 3.1). God intended that Jill have a baby; otherwise she would not have become pregnant. The argument that sexual relations (and not God's wish) result in pregnancies is not convincing for many believers since they know that a pregnancy does not result every time a woman has sex.

This description of the complete acceptance of a "divinity that shapes our ends, rough-hew them how we will" (Shakespeare) may fit the religious ideology of some believers, but certainly does *not* fit the values of most religious people. It does describe the stereotype that some secular social workers have of religious groups, but it misses the actual value stance of most. Many secular social workers tend to agree with the characterization of religion as "a kind of spiritual intoxicant" and with the assessment that "religion teaches those who toil in poverty all their lives to be resigned and patient in this world, and console themselves with the hope of reward in heaven" (Lenin 1940:11). They are convinced that the truly religious are complete fatalists.

There is a basis for this characterization in the Lutheran tradition which expounded a model of obedience that demanded that every person subordinate all desires to those of the superior. In effect, this Lutheran model denied free will and active participation to all but the secular ruler. Complete submission to the ruler, even if he was a tyrant, was demanded of everyone. According to Luther, "even if those in authority are evil or without faith, nevertheless the authority and its power is good and from God" (1931:82). Total submission to the Commandments and to God's representative on earth was posited as a supreme value. But in practice few religious people, even Lutherans, accept this extreme fatalistic position.

All religions provide for a measure of free will—some more and some less. Interesting in this connection is Halevy's thought that blind acceptance of God's control applies only to past events, while people themselves have full responsibility for their current and future choices (1983 2:244–45). Maimonides noted that "the mission of the Prophets and the giving of the Law would have been altogether superfluous" if people did not have the power to make choices (1956:325). By incorporating the value of free will, as most theologians have done, individuals have been charged with responsibility for what they are and what they can become. Only the individual can be an effective change "agent"—no one else can take responsibility for what he or she makes out of life.

The mainstream of social work ideology makes no assumptions about the causes of problems. Instead, problems may be the result of environmental system flaws, individual inadequacies, or a combination of both. Yet for social workers who base their practice on the psychiatric or on the Marxian model, deterministic explanations figure prominently. These explanations tend to relieve people of moral culpability. For example, when it is believed that criminal behavior is caused solely by the consequences of the capitalistic system, there is little that the criminal can do to mend his ways as long as that system continues to exist. This approach means, more often than not, that social workers assume that a person is the victim of a problem situation for which he or she bears little or no responsibility. If this is the case, a person can hardly be expected to control his or her fate, though such an approach need not deny altogether a client's capacity to do something about his or her predicament.

But in practice, social workers generally tone down the more deterministic elements of any theory they use. For example, Freud's death concept (*thanatos*) was dropped by most of those who have accepted his theory of ego psychology. Similarly, most radical social workers have abandoned the more deterministic elements of orthodox structural Marxism in favor of a less deterministic Hegelian version. Social workers who practice behavior modification have substituted a more moral and more voluntaristic form of behaviorism for the stark model of Walden II Skinnerism. As Philp remarked so concisely, "Essentially, any theory which suggests forces permanently beyond the individual's control is either ignored by, or subverted to, social work's regime of truth" (1979:93). The secular social work ideology does not discount responsibility for decisions altogether. People have some control over their fate, even while in many situations individuals are the victims of forces beyond their control.

In fact, most social workers, both religious and secular, have chosen a middle position which combines free will and determinism. This nondogmatic, pragmatic position has been called "soft determinism" (Reamer 1983). However, there may be shades of difference between secular and religious social workers who follow the soft determinism approach. What difference, if any, does it make whether a given social worker follows a more or a less deterministic model of practice? Reamer has suggested that the stronger the commitment to determinism, the greater the social worker's emphasis on the social change approach, while the stronger the commitment to individual autonomy and free will, the greater the emphasis on the casework approach (1983:641). To what extent this logical deduction is in consonance with reality needs further empirical testing.

However, the values that a social worker holds are not the only factor that must be considered. Many clients have been raised in cultures that reinforce a strong belief in predestination and fate. These clients tend to doubt that their problem can be solved through their own efforts. Social workers may experience difficulties when trying to apply professional concepts such as client self-determination with these clients. This problem can be especially trying for social workers in developing countries, but it is also familiar to American social workers whose clients come from deprived backgrounds (Adler and Midgley 1978).

Part II

Practice Issues and Dilemmas for Social Workers

Chapter Four

Religion and Values
in Social Work Practice

The religious belief (or lack of belief) of a chemist does not mean anything to the molecules, atoms, or electrons that he explores. An architect's religious beliefs (or lack of beliefs) does not affect the design of a building that he drafts. Nor will the accountant who regularly attends church prepare one sort of profit/loss statement and his agnostic colleague another. But the religious beliefs of social workers may have meaning and relevance for those with whom they interact. And these religious beliefs (or lack of them) may influence what they do as practitioners.

The propositions discussed in the last chapter would lead us to expect some differences in the social work practice patterns and decisions of religious social workers, when these are compared with those of their nonreligious or secular colleagues. These differences, we would assume, will be more obvious (and perhaps more problematic) the greater the commitment and the deeper the workers' beliefs.

In the first section of this chapter I will briefly review several studies that have examined the question of possible differences that religion might make for social work practice. Next I will look at the efficacy of client-worker value matching; does value congruence lead to more effective outcomes? The central role of values, particularly religious values, demands that we analyze the problem of how social workers avoid imposing their values on clients, even while being true to their own values. I will examine in the final section of this chapter various ways in which social workers have attempted to reconcile their religious beliefs with professional social work values.

Comparing Religious and Secular Social Workers

It is undoubtedly an oversimplification of a very complex reality to categorize thousands of professional social workers into two groups according to their religious belief or nonbelief. Such a dichotomy is inaccurate because not all believers are alike, just as not all nonbelievers are. There are many different degrees of belief, just as there are many different shades of nonbelief. We can find among social workers, just as among all Americans, people holding a great variety of differing religious beliefs and nonbeliefs and observing a wide range of religious practices and rituals. Those not committed to or identified with any organized religion may hold strong beliefs in humanism, univeralism, social justice, or one of a number of idea systems that attract a high level of commitment. It is not my task here to assess these belief systems, but as in earlier chapters I will continue to use the concept of religious belief more narrowly to identify those who are committed to one of the belief systems of organized Western religion, especially Christianity and Judaism. But I will also include in my definition of religious social workers those who are associated with any of the branches of the Muslim religion, as well as the followers of various Eastern religions. Given this definition, it may be helpful for analytical purposes to dichotomize the social worker population. I will first review the relevant literature, even though it is very sparse.

Eckardt, in an empirical study (1974), compared two groups of social work students who were very different in their religious backgrounds and beliefs. One group was composed of evangelical Christians who studied social work at a Bible college, while the second group was composed of secular and liberal Christians who attended a school of social work at a state university. Despite these differences in religious backgrounds he found that members of both groups were similar in terms of their professional identity and practice decisions. Even though there are major differences between the values proclaimed by evangelical Christianity and those attributed to professional social work, Eckardt did not discover any essential differences in the professional practice of religious and secular social workers. Respondents from both groups, when presented with critical incidents taken from social work practice, indicated positive affirmation of such professional values as client self-determination and worker trust in client. Members of both groups also affirmed the value of individual-society mutuality. There were minor differences but essential agreement between the two groups with regard to their belief in the client's capacity to change. Eckardt concluded that "the overwhelming difference in religious beliefs was matched by an equally overwhelming similarity of practice" (1974:215).

Eckardt's findings did not support the proposition that a worker's religious beliefs have a major impact on his or her practice. It may well be that the choice of incidents led to this finding. Most of the practice situations tested were taken from what may be called "the zone of indifference," that is, from the type of practice problems where specific religious values either do not give direction or coincide with the corresponding secular values. Practice situations for which one can expect major differences between religious and secular social workers, such as problems involving abortion, homosexuality, and premarital sex, were not tested in Eckardt's study. The finding that there is consensus does not necessarily mean that religious social workers will always practice in the same manner as their secular colleagues. Had Eckardt tested more "critical" incidents, he might well have found that religious beliefs do have an impact on social work practice.

Earlier Frey (1973) had found that most social work students in her study did not attach any great importance to their religious beliefs. Her findings also did not indicate any differences in the casework practice of secular and religious social workers. The only statistically significant difference reported occurred when religiously oriented workers practiced with religious clients. Religious social workers generally assessed the religious involvement of their clients in a much more positive way than did their secular colleagues. They also had a higher expectation of behavioral changes for religious clients.

Frey also noted that secular social workers made more frequent referrals to the clergy than did religious social workers. This might suggest that religiously oriented social workers may be more comfortable in handling the religious aspects of a problem situation as part of the total problem, while their secular colleagues referred these same problems to religious specialists. This hypothesis would be in line with the findings of a number of other studies that reported that secular therapists do not tend to define client problems in spiritual terms and avoid goals that concern clients' spiritual lives, even when clients are religious and their beliefs do play a very important part in their lives (O'Leary and Wilson 1975; Ginsburg 1950; Worthington and Scott 1983). At the same time, it is becoming increasingly clear that secular social workers and therapists cannot avoid altogether the subject of religion when this is an important factor in their clients' lives.

The Religious Factor in Social Work Practice

The proposition that religious values influence social work practice received partial confirmation in a preliminary study I participated in recently (Baum et al. 1987). In this study it was found that there are specific practice areas (including abortion, homosexuality, and euthanasia) where religious values do make a difference, especially when these involve practitioner or client behaviors that seem to violate these values and beliefs. In these situations, religious values do impact on the practice of many social workers. In other practice areas social workers evidently are influenced more by professional or secular values and norms than by religious values.

These findings are similar to those reported in a study of 1,729 American Christians. The analysis of data from this nationwide probability sample showed that the impact of religious beliefs was essentially limited to the domains of family life, sexuality, and personal honesty (Hoge and DeZulueta 1985).

Evidently religious values are only one of several sources of influence on social work practice. Social workers, even religiously oriented social workers, are also influenced by the cultural values of the general society in which they live, by professional social work values, and by the demands and policies of the agencies in which they practice. Which of these four sets of value criteria is most influential at any given instance depends most probably on the specificity, clarity, and strength of the relevant value. For example, when a religious value is specific and perceived as unambiguous, as in the case of the opposition to euthanasia, those social workers who have indicated an attachment to religious values are clearly influenced and guided by it. On the other hand, when a religious value is not perceived so clearly or when it is believed that this value has been subject to various differing interpretations, as in the case of the prohibition of the use of contraceptive procedures, even religiously attached social workers are often more influenced by secular and professional values which come through more forcefully and less ambiguously.

Religious values concerning abortion are another example that suggests that every person, not only social workers, is influenced by a number of different values. In our preliminary study, almost half of the religious social worker respondents were willing to help a client obtain an abortion, even though such a request appeared to be contrary to religious precepts. This practice behavior may be based on the professional value which supports a client's right to make her own decision or on the recognition that abortion is culturally and legally permissible in our society. The response of our research sample was not too different from the response Gallup reported in a more recent nationwide poll. Forty-five percent of the Gallup poll respondents favored the 1973 Supreme Court ruling that a woman may obtain an abortion anytime during the first three months of pregnancy. Even among Catholics, 41 percent favored this position. Two out of every three Southern Baptists, on the other hand, opposed this approach (Gallup 1986:18). The positive response, both in the Gallup poll and in our preliminary research (Baum et al. 1987) does not necessarily mean that the respondents would decide for an abortion for themselves, but that they would respect such a request from another person, such as a client.

But the significance of religion in social work practice goes far beyond the practice of those who are formally identified as religious. Workers who are not religious, who style themselves as secular or humanist or even atheist, may not think that religion makes much of a difference in their practice. They may even believe that religion is an illusion or that it represents an irrational and infantile behavior. Yet when they work with clients who believe and for whom religion is a central part of their lives, the religious factor will make a difference. Ignoring or deliberately avoiding this segment of a client's life will inevitably create problems in the professional relationship between client and social worker.

Client-Worker Matching

One of the basic assumptions of social worker practice is that a person interacts with another as a whole person. Deliberately avoiding one segment of a person's life, such as religion, will handicap the interaction, even if it is a professional relationship between a social worker and a client. One may wonder whether a social worker can really have a meaningful or helpful relationship with clients who have a strong religious commitment when such a social worker avoids the religious aspects of their lives altogether.

Problems may occur when clients and social workers hold different religious values or follow different religious practices. The situation may be even more problematic when one of the two believes and the other does not. As Goldstein (1986) noted, "the initiation of any substantial relationship (including the helping relationship) depends on the extent to which its members can share, compliment, or otherwise resolve their moral differences." The lack of spiritual sharing may be the source of a major problem in social work. This is especially so because, according to two prominent social work educators, there exists a "major discrepancy between the anti-religious and non-religious attitudes of mental health professionals and the religious beliefs, values and practices of a large proportion of clients" (Siporin and Glasser 1987:24).

What kinds of problems can arise when client and social worker differ in their approaches to religion? Gass (1984) examined the religious beliefs, values, and expectations for therapy of orthodox Christian college students and compared these with those of nonorthodox Christian and non-Christian college students. He found that orthodox Christians had a distinct and different set of values relating to the goals and procedures of the therapeutic process. When faced by emotional distress, they expressed definite preferences for certain specific coping mechanisms. They also expressed considerable concern over the religious orientation of a prospective therapist. Nonorthodox students, on the other hand, identified different criteria for therapeutic goals and procedures, preferred other coping methods, and were not concerned with the religious orientation of their therapist.

These differences are important and may have implications for social work practice, but do not permit us to conclude that it is necessarily desirable for client and worker to have identical religious beliefs. There may be other ways in which social workers can overcome a client-worker value discrepancy. Practitioners who are sensitive to the role that religion plays in their clients' lives may be successful, even when they themselves are not believers. Thus, Humphries thought that the different philosophies of life of clients and workers would not interfere with successful therapy "as long as the therapist remains conscious that religious issues are not reducible to psychological problems or defenses" (1982:129). But there are those who have suggested that a consensus between client and worker concerning religious values is desirable because it tends to increase the chances for successful outcomes.

A client's confidence in his or her social worker is almost a prerequisite for successful goal achievement (Loewenberg 1983:178—85). Confidence or faith in the "healer" may be as important if not more important than any other aspect of the helping process (Frank 1972). This is an especially crucial consideration when serving frightened and dependent people, which many social work clients are. A mutual attraction on the basis of shared values may optimize this confidence and thus maximize the opportunity for a successful outcome of the helping encounter (Kadushin and Wieringa 1960).

But in the real world of social work practice, religious value matching is not always possible, even if it is thought to be desirable. Instead, various combinations will occur; none is without its problems and challenges. My analysis in this section is based, in part, on McMinn's earlier work (1984). A simplified dichotomy of values into religious and secular values will result in a paradigm of four possible client–social worker relationships, as in table 4.1 These are pure or "ideal" types which exaggerate reality in order to highlight differences. Such a fourfold schema slights important differences between various types of religious value positions (e.g., fundamentalist, orthodox, and liberal), just as it overlooks differences between various secular value positions (e.g., humanist, agnostic, atheist, antireligious). It also ignores the reality that most persons do not respond to only one monolithic value set, be it religious or secular. In actual life, almost everybody responds to a variety of value sets, both secular and religious. Some of the values that a person holds may even be conflicting. I

TABLE 4.1. Typology of Client–Social Worker Value Relationship

		Client's Values	
		Religious	Secular
Social Worker's Values	Religious	1	2
	Secular	3	4

noted earlier how this multiexposure may result in some religious social workers making seemingly secular practice decisions and some secular social workers accepting practice decisions that seem to be influenced by religious values. Yet worker-client value complementarity does seem to make for greater effectiveness.

I will first present a vignette that will be used later to examine the implications of the different client-worker relationships identified in the above display.

Case 4.1. Gladys Cheats on Her Husband

Gladys Rauf, twenty-six years old, is an elementary school teacher. She is married to Peter Rauf, age twenty-seven, who is a certified public accountant. They have been married for three years and do not have any children. Mrs. Rauf was referred to the social worker by her physician because she complained of constant headaches for which there appeared to be no physical cause.

In an early session with the social worker, Gladys spoke about her childhood. She was raised in a traditional home where religious values were always stressed. She attended church regularly until a year and a half ago; then she suddenly stopped going to church. She could not or would not tell the social worker why she stopped attending church.

In a later session Gladys Rauf hinted that she and her husband did not have good sexual relations. However, when pressed, she indicated that she was not ready to explore this matter with the social worker. Several weeks later she revealed that she has been having several extramarital affairs in the last year and a half. She broke off each relationship because she felt guilty about cheating on her husband, who has been good to her. But before long, somehow or other, for no evident reason, she drifted into yet another affair. And each time her headaches got worse.

Before analyzing this vignette we must recognize that not everybody who is involved in an extramarital affair will feel guilty, nor will everyone who "cheats" on a spouse have headaches. At the same time we should keep in mind that among many groups in the population the traditional sanctions against adultery are maintained in full force. Others, though no longer constrained by these traditional moral controls, have not yet learned how to cope with the dilemmas that arise out of the newer life-styles.

A social worker whose practice decisions are guided by religious values (this type of social worker will henceforth be abbreviated as SWr) will most likely define Gladys's problem in terms of deviant behavior and identify a change in that behavior as a desirable goal. This social worker will attempt to help the client discontinue the disvalued behavior. It is expected that as a result of a behavioral change from extramarital affairs to marital fidelity the client will feel less guilty and will have fewer headaches. On the other hand, a social worker whose practice decisions are based primarily on secular values may identify Gladys' guilt as the problem that must be corrected. This type of social worker will be abbreviated as SWs. The first goal of the SWs will be to reduce the damaging guilt feelings without necessarily trying to achieve any behavioral changes. This social worker may help relieve the guilt feelings by counseling Gladys to have better sexual relations within marriage so as to remove the need for guilt-producing extramarital activities. Or SWs may attempt to relieve the guilt feelings in some other ways that do not involve ending the extramarital activities. But the important objective for SWs is to relieve the guilt feelings, since these are always undesirable. SWs may disapprove of adultery as much as SWr, but the former is less likely to emphasize behavioral changes as a goal of choice.

This is how the situation might look to two different social workers. The client also will define her problem in terms of how she sees the world in which she lives. She will assess the social worker's suggestions and questions in terms of her own frame of reference. The client who has a religious value base will have one set of expectations, while the client with a secular value base will have another. We will call the first client Cr and the second, Cs. Each will respond to the social worker in a different manner and will assess "success" in a way that is congruent with his or her particular value approach.

I will examine next, in greater detail, the impact on practice of each of the four combinations identified in table 4.1. Again I must caution that this model, like all models in science, grossly oversimplifies a very complex reality to make a point. In reality there is neither one type of SWr nor one type of SWs; instead there are many shades of combinations that are represented in this analysis by four ideal types.

TYPE 1: RELIGIOUS CLIENT, RELIGIOUS SOCIAL WORKER:

Some religious people try to avoid social workers and other human service professionals altogether. They believe that such help is "satanic" or they think that by turning to a professional for help they indicate a lack of trust in God. Some may even be afraid that they will be exposed to a kind of secular brainwashing if they become a social agency client (Rayburn 1985:37–38). But when both client and worker share common religious values, these concerns and fears are minimized. Value congruence may facilitate agreement on goals and strategies. Client motivation to participate in the helping process will be relatively strong when both client and worker share a common value approach.

The probability is high that this client will continue in the helping relationship until the goal has been achieved. Gladys Rauf may or may not be aware of a connection between her extramarital affairs and her headaches. But she is very conscious that guilt feelings occur whenever she cheats on her husband. Guilt, among other things, is an indicator of not accepting one's current behavior. A person who cannot accept own behavior will want to change it, but so far Gladys has not been successful in doing so. She pleads for help in changing her "sinful" behavior. SWr will tend to agree with this assessment and will try help the client along the requested lines.

This combination, where worker and client share common religious values and beliefs, is thought by many to be the most desirable match. However, in this situation it is important that SWr remember that he or she is a social worker and not a religious functionary. There is a potential danger that some SWr social workers will take on "the mantle of psychological as well as spiritual authority" (Stern 1985:11). Another danger is that a religious social worker may overidentify with a client whose spiritual struggles are reminiscent of the worker's own experiences. Such unacknowledged overidentification may result in assessment mistakes and intervention errors (Peteet 1981). There also may be a temptation to argue about minor doctrinal interpretations or to impose solutions by appealing to scriptural sources. Some religious clients may try to avoid facing painful revelations by attempting to argue with their social workers about doctrine. The social worker in such situations must assume responsibility for focusing on the professional helping relationship and for not engaging in activities that are not relevant to this end.

TYPE 2: SECULAR CLIENT, RELIGIOUS SOCIAL WORKER

This client may expect that the social worker will help reduce her guilt feelings but does not want any intervention that is designed to change her behavior. Even if Gladys Rauf desires to change her behavior, she may not see any connection between the behavior and her headaches. The religious social worker, on the other hand, will define the problem and identify the goals in other ways, as discussed above for type 1. The secular client may not understand how the attempt to change her behavior will help reduce her headaches. SWr must be aware that different value orientations may lead to disagreement on goals and/or strategies and that such a disagreement may result in a potential stalemate. Even if open conflict is avoided, the client's participation in the helping process may be minimal and her motivation may not be sufficiently strong to fully involve her in the change efforts. Under such circumstances, the chances for a successful outcome will be low.

Another possibility is that SWr will try to help this client to redefine the problem. One way to achieve this is to attempt to influence the client's value structure so that this client will change from Cs to Cr. However, there are serious questions about the ethical propriety of social workers engaging in this type of intervention activity. While social workers always "influence" clients, this particularly type of worker activity is akin to proselytism, which is more appropriate for an evangelist or a missionary than for a social worker. Even though religious social workers may be convinced of the correctness of their religious beliefs, the professional ethics clearly demand that they avoid proselytism. Additional problems that religiously oriented social workers may encounter in working with secular clients, especially the problem of "cooperation," will be discussed in chapter 5.

TYPE 3: RELIGIOUS CLIENT, SECULAR SOCIAL WORKER

This client is somewhat aware that her guilt feelings are connected with her unfaithful sexual behavior. She probably expects help in changing this behavior. The SWs social worker may or may not see a connection between the adulterous behavior and the guilt feelings, but will be inclined to focus attention first on reducing the disabling guilt feelings.

SWs should be aware that whenever the client and the social worker have different approaches, there may be disagreement about goals and/or strategies. When such a disagreement does occur, the client may not participate fully in the helping process. Even if she does participate, her motivation may not be sufficiently strong for goal achievement. Given these circumstances a successful outcome will be less than likely.

Some social workers in the Cr-SWs combination may attempt to reduce the disabling guilt feelings by initiating a change in the client's value system from religious to secular. These social workers may assume that their own rational humanist values are far superior to the irrational religious values of the client. They essentially agree with the idea that "the values of the psychotherapist [are] more carefully reasoned and, on the whole, more adequate than the values of the general public" (Walls 1980:641). Social workers who take this stance must consider carefully the ethical implications of imposing their own values on clients, even when they do so only indirectly, by making suggestions or by implication. Placing the worker's own values above those of the client is rarely justified. Such an attitude may interfere with an accurate assessment of the problem. In addition, workers should consider the interpersonal tensions and dysphoria that may result from a successful attempt to change a client's religious values without at the same time making sure of the backing of a strong and pervasive social support system that will be able to reinforce these new values.

Missionary activities must be avoided by all social workers, no matter whether their orientation is religious or humanist or radical. There is no reason to assume that SWs proselytism is any more justified than SWr proselytism. Some social workers have suggested that one way to keep these problems from occurring even unintentionally is by disclosing their own values to the client at the very first opportunity in the first session. Such a knowledge will help the client to evaluate properly what the social worker is saying. But early self-disclosure may be damaging for some clients, especially if they feel that the worker is challenging their own basic values when these are quite different from those of the worker (Beit-Hallahmi 1975).

There may be occasions when changing a client's values is the goal of choice, but the choice should be made both by the client and the social worker. Effecting value changes, directly or indirectly, without the client's full and informed consent is a violation of the NASW *Code of Ethics* and is not acceptable social work practice. Attempts to impose a value change are probably rare since most social workers are aware that this is an unprofessional and unethical activity. More frequent may be the situation where an SWs who is not aware of the value mismatch may inadvertently "impose" his or her secular values by identifying the guilt feelings, rather than the behavior, as the major problem. The message that this social worker sends is that there is nothing wrong with extramarital relations, as long as these are satisfying. While this social worker may not be guilty of intentional unethical conduct, the results of his or her unintentional actions may be just as damaging, especially if the client believes that adulterous relations are wrong.

TYPE 4: SECULAR CLIENT, SECULAR SOCIAL WORKER

In this combination both client and social worker share similar values so that the professional and ethical problems discussed for types 2 and 3 will not arise. As in type 1, value congruence will facilitate agreement on goals and strategies. Both client and worker will focus on activities designed to reduce the guilt feelings. Client motivation will be relatively high and there is a good probability that this client will continue to participate actively until the agreed-to goal has been achieved.

DISCUSSION

The typology presented here is purposefully simplistic. Like all models in science, the model is a heuristic device designed to reduce a very complicated matter into something simple in order to highlight one or two elements. The real world is not so simple. There is neither a monolithic religious value set nor a unitary secular value set. Furthermore, value congruence between worker and client while desirable, does not guarantee success. When there is value congruence, there may still be conflict or disagreement around a wide variety of topics. The value discrepancy in some "congruent" combinations may be greater than in some of the mismatched combinations. For example, the value mismatch between a religious evangelical person and a religious liberal person may be greater than between the values held by a liberal churchgoer and a humanist agnostic.

The actual value matching will be characterized by many practical problems, even if one is convinced of its desirability. How does one go about "typing" the religious/secular values of clients and workers? Even if we were successful in developing a valid instrument for value typing, it will not always be possible to come up with a social worker of just the right "type." Perhaps the more important lesson that can be drawn from this analysis is that social workers in the mismatched combinations (types 2 and 3) must accept responsibility for making certain that the value discrepancy will not interfere unduly with the helping process. The first step in doing this is an objective assessment of one's own value profile and the value profile of the client.

Value Judgments and Value Imposition

It is a widely accepted principle that a social worker must be value neutral. Thus, when discussing the requirements for counseling pregnant teenagers, one author wrote that "a social worker must maintain a neutral position if she is to help the girl choose among the various options" available to her (Cain 1979:53). Even though the *Code of Ethics* of the National Association of Social Workers (1980) does not contain a specific paragraph that requires the suspension of the workers' value judgments, one of the core professional expectations is that social workers do not impose their own personal values on clients and that they suspend judgment about clients' behaviors and actions, even when their own values or societal values demand a judgment (DeFelicia 1982).

This requirement for avoiding values was introduced in the social sciences almost a century ago by Max Weber. Freud excluded values as a consideration in therapy and laid down the value of "no value." Value neutrality has become a cardinal value of all occupational groups that claim professional status. However, value neutrality (as it is generally interpreted) is virtually impossible for social workers, no matter whether they hold religious, secular, or other values.

When Gladys Rauf (case 4.1) told her social worker that she felt guilty about engaging in extramarital sex, and the worker dealt with her *guilt* as the problem, the worker was expressing just as much of a value judgment about extramarital sex as another worker would when he or she condemned adultery. The social worker who counseled Carl (case 3.2) concerning his ambivalent feelings about homosexual relations could not help but express a value judgment about homosexuality. If he indicated that it did not matter whether a person preferred gay or straight sex, he would have expressed just as much a value judgment as he would have had he indicated that heterosexual relations are preferable from a societal or moral viewpoint. The social worker who assisted Jill (case 3.1) to obtain an abortion was no more value neutral than a collegue who was determined to help her decide not to have an abortion. The professional expectation that demands that a worker not be judgmental but instead be value neutral was developed in reaction to what was perceived by many social workers as the paternalistic moralism, that was characteristic of early charity workers. But value neutrality may be just as moralistic as the earlier paternalism.

Many say that all moralistic judgments are undesirable in social work practice, no matter whether they are based on religious or secular values. At the same time, value neutrality may not only be undesirable and ineffective, it may even be damaging. Maslow noted that "the classical philosophy of science as morally neutral, value free, value neutral is not only wrong, but is extremely dangerous" (1969:724). Similarly, Glasser said that in social work the nonjudgmental approach may lead "to a practice that at best is not helpful to our clients and at worst can be quite harmful to them. . . . the worker has both the right and the obligation to place the client's decision-making process in a moral context" (1984:8). Others have suggested that the value-free rule is a rule that neither can nor should be implemented in social work practice. Pilseker, for example, wrote that "social workers cannot be nonjudgmental and they should not attempt to be so. They are merchants of morality and should acknowledge this fact openly instead of talking as if they believed that 'anything goes' " (1978:55).

VALUE NEUTRALITY IS A VALUE

An even more severe indictment of the value-neutral rule was presented by Salomon when she wrote that for social workers the insistence on value neutrality is itself a value. According to her, it is

a kind of de facto ideology—one that is insidious, because unacknowledged; one that permits moralistic judgments by the very caseworker who eschews "judgmentalism." . . . The caseworker may, without awareness, judge a compulsively tidy housewife as severely as his 19th century predecessor judged a slovenly one. (1967:30)

Value neutrality is itself a value, a value that may be more insidious than others because it does not appear openly as a value. When social workers say that they exclude values from professional considerations, they tend to ignore the impact of their own values on their practice without really diminishing the effect of those values. According to Humphries (1982), this "constitutes an area of potential abuse" because denying one's own values does not make it possible to consider any safeguards to avoid harming clients.

JUDGEMENTALISM AND RELIGIOUS VALUES

Judgmentalism can be defined as evaluating or assessing another person's behavior or opinions on the basis of one's own values. Judgmentalism is based on the assumption that only one's own values are valid or that they are far superior to all other values. Value neutrality, on the other hand, can be defined as evaluating or assessing another person's behavior or opinions without reference to any values because it is held that values are not relevant to the scientific process. Unrestrained judgmentalism may interfere with effective social work practice. But it may be possible to suspend or limit judgmentalism without requiring value neutrality. A social worker who avoids unrestrained judgmentalism is not necessarily indifferent to the moral implications of what a client does or says. Neither is such a worker required to condone everything a client does. When we say that a social worker should avoid unrestrained judgmentalism, we refer to the way in which that worker should use his or her values in the professional interaction, but without imposing them on the client.

It has been said that religious values require religiously committed social workers to be judgmental, but this need not be so. It is, of course, true that religion has been used (or misused) to defend judgmentalism and paternalism. A long series of sermons from the seventeenth and eighteenth centuries, and even from more recent times, can be cited to support this viewpoint. This is what Keith-Lucas had in mind when he noted, "Although judgmentalism has been one of the greatest sins of the church, the Christian view on man's situation can also be a source of exactly the opposite" (1960:89). Biestek (1953), a noted social work educator and a Jesuit priest, clearly rejected both judgmentalism and value neutrality. Religion does not require unrestrained judgmentalism; religious social workers need not be judgmental.

Writing from a secular perspective, Titmuss also noted that social work can never be value free. Though his focus was on social policy, his observations apply to all methods of social work practice.

We all have our values and our prejudices. . . . At the very least, we have a responsibility for making our values clear; and we have a special duty to do so when we are discussing such a subject as social policy which, quite clearly, has no meaning at all if it is considered to be neutral in terms of values. (1974:27)

It is not realistic to expect social workers not to "judge"; no person can be indifferent to what others do. According to Menninger, a social worker's life-style will usually reveal his or her position on moral issues, even when these are not declared publicly (1973:215). More than that, the person who denies his or her own values tends to lack authenticity, and authenticity and honesty are crucial attributes for the truly effective helper.

PROTECTING CLIENTS FROM UNRESTRAINED JUDGMENTALISM

Yet how can a social worker protect clients from the inevitable judgmentalism? Instead of making an impossible demand, that social workers not be judgmental, we should consider a number of practice strategies that might safeguard against the potential abuse of unrestrained judgmentalism. The following are some of the ways that have been suggested:

Judging Clients/Evaluating Behavior. In one of the earliest considerations of this problem area in the social work literature, Biestek recommended that social workers refrain "from judging the guilt or innocence of the client [but] objectively judge the attitudes, standards, or actions of the client." He felt that judging a client would be harmful but that evaluating his or her behavior would not necessarily hurt the client (1953:237). Though this advice has been repeated by a number of social work authors, it has, to the best of my knowledge, never been determined empirically whether the suggested distinction does make a difference in the social work situation. The distinction between judging a person and judging that person's behavior may not be critical for effective practice. Biestek's strategy was derived from the parent-child relationship. When there is a long-term healthy, loving relationship between two people, this relation will not be disturbed when one person criticizes or evaluates a specific behavior of the other. However, the professional social work encounter is a short-term relationship that focuses on a specific problem. How meaningful will it be in this situation to differentiate between judging the person and evaluating his or her behavior? Further research is needed to answer this question.

Suspending Judgment. It may be helpful for the social worker to suspend judgment for a time in order to establish a more effective helping relationship with a client. This may be difficult when working with a client who by his or her behavior takes issue with everything the religiously committed social worker considers sacred. This is especially difficult when the client is (or was once) identified with the same church or sect as is the worker. The situation may be just as difficult for the highly committed humanist social worker whose client engages in religious activities that have little meaning for this secular social worker. In all of these instances, social workers will make value judgments because they cannot deny their own values. But these workers should learn to suspend their judgment temporarily in order to begin to engage in a helpful and professional relationship.

Power Equalization. Value judgments are potentially dangerous and especially harmful when they are linked with power (Herskovitz

1947:76). In the social work encounter, the social worker is usually more powerful than the client. Safeguards can be instituted by adopting practice strategies that are designed to correct this power imbalance. One way is to discuss the worker's values and beliefs with the client, openly and candidly. By doing so, the worker gives to the client the power of choice. Instead of covertly influencing him or her to adopt the worker's beliefs and values, this open approach suggests that the worker's value system is only one out of many available choices (Humphries 1982; Judah 1985). But as I noted already, Beit-Hallahmi (1975) cautioned against the routine disclosure of worker's beliefs. He felt that in many instances such a procedure would have more negative than positive consequences.

In His Own Image. For the religiously committed person there is another strategy that may provide safeguards against harm resulting from value judgments. The person who believes in God also believes that "God created man in His own image" (Genesis 1:27). God created *all* persons in his own image, sinner as well as saint. Even those whose current behavior may be "deviant" were created in his image. As one writer stated, "In this outcast, in this adulterer, in this homosexual . . . there is still enough to make a saint" (Stern 1985:5). In this approach one does not differentiate between the person and his or her behavior. Instead, every person is accepted because he or she was created in God's image. It is believed that the expression of value judgments about the person's behavior will strengthen rather than harm the encounter because these values are said to reflect a total love and respect for the divine spark that is thought to be in every human being.

NON-CHRISTIAN CLIENTS

Working with clients who have not accepted Jesus may be a problem for some Christian social workers, especially for those who interpret literally the biblical command not to have fellowship with the world (Ephesians 6.17). The obligation to do good to all (Galatians 6.10) and to minister in love to all who are in need (Luke 10.30–37) provides support for those who are ready to work with all persons, no matter what their beliefs. The dilemma faced by the first group may be more sociological than theological. A dozen scriptural verses will mean little to persons whose reference group severely disapproves of contact with strangers or with nonbelievers. Such social workers may not find it possible to function in settings other than those that provide service only to members of their own denomination.

Missionaries attempt to proselytize for their religion and to win souls for their faith, but social workers must remember that they are not missionaries. They must not use the authority of their professional role to impose their values and their beliefs, religious or other, on clients. The operating term here is "impose." In the client-worker relationship there is always a power imbalance. Clients often come from powerless social groups, while social workers usually represent the powerful establishment. There are some situations where initially the client may have more power than the worker, but even these powerful clients often lose part of their power by revealing to the social worker the most private parts of their personal lives or by sharing with the worker potentially damaging information about themselves or their families. Social workers must not take advantage of this weakness and impose their own values.

CLIENTS' RIGHT TO REJECT ADVICE

A basic proposition of social work practice is that every client has the right to reject the advice or plan presented by the social worker. This proposition applies to all situations, whether or not it involves religious aspects. However, social workers need to be aware that client dependency varies with the value of the benefits received. The greater the benefit that the client derives from the social worker or from the social agency, the greater the likelihood that the client will become increasingly dependent upon the social worker; at the very least, such a client is not likely to disagree with the social worker and thereby risk the social worker's disapproval and the possibility of forfeiting the benefits. It is not important that a responsible social worker would not act in such a punitive manner; what is important is that many clients *believe* that the worker would do so.

One empirical study of social work services in England found that clients felt relatively free to reject professional advice when they were receiving only "talking therapy" but they felt less free to reject the worker's advice when they also received valuable concrete services, such as health care (Handler and Hollingsworth 1971). Making the receipt of financial aid or other concrete help dependent on accepting a social worker's "advice" denies clients the right to make their own decisions. Generally, social workers honor this right; however, there are situations where, perhaps unwittingly, this right is ignored or limited. Standardized budgets may make it impossible for Muslim or Jewish client's to observe their dietary laws. Administrative requirements may create obstacles for unemployed Sabbath observers. Social workers must be alert to safeguard every client's right of choice.

There are those who have argued that all clients, both those with a religious orientation and those with a secular one, should have the right to request a social worker with a similar religious (or nonreligious) viewpoint. Otherwise there is the danger that "therapy may become an exercise in proselytism without consent," even when the social worker does not have any such intentions (McMinn 1984:3). There may be administrative problems in implementing such a policy; however, although for many clients religious matching may not be important, for some, especially for the religiously more committed ones, it is very important. Whenever possible, a client's feelings in this matter should be taken into consideration. Value matching will tend to reduce the problem of value imposition, but it will not eliminate it because rarely, if ever, do two persons share exactly the same values and adhere to them to the same degree. A fuller discussion of the issues involved in value matching was presented earlier in this chapter.

RECONCILING RELIGIOUS BELIEFS AND
PROFESSIONAL VALUES

There are times when a social worker's religious beliefs seem to be in conflict with the value orientation of the profession. For some social workers this conflict does not exist because they have given clear priority to one or the other value set. But for other social workers specific practice situations like the one described in case 4.2 may pose a problem. One author wrote, "The value of self-determination causes problems for the evangelical social worker because he believes that choices . . . people [make] are often contrary to God who is good and [who] knows what is best" (Eckardt 1974:205). How can a religious social worker reconcile his or her religious beliefs with the professional ideology when there is a conflict between the two?

Many religiously committed social workers are keenly aware that there is a discontinuity between the spiritually neutral professional theories and the religious values in which they believe. Eckardt recalls "vividly the tensions and problems which developed as I sought to integrate my evangelical Christian faith with professional identity and practice. At times the struggle was almost overwhelming when there seemed to be no common ground which could support both identities simultaneously" (1974:iii).

I will utilize an actual practice situation to illustrate various strategies that social workers have evolved to reconcile such conflicting value sets.

Case 4.2: This Pregnancy Was a Mistake
Darlene Porter is a twenty-seven-year-old married woman, and the mother of two children. She is again pregnant, and has asked for help in arranging an abortion. Neither she nor her husband want any more children. This pregnancy was a mistake. She had forgotten to take her birth control pills.

Conflict between religious beliefs and professional practice values is not limited to evangelical Christians, but has been reported by workers coming from a wide variety of religious backgrounds. Not every religious social worker experiences this conflict with the same intensity. Nor is every such conflict necessarily a negative or damaging experience. Coser, for example, noted that from a societal point of view segmental participation and role conflict can produce a "kind of balancing mechanism, preventing deep cleavages along one axis" (1956:78–80). Yet every social worker who experiences a "conflict" between religious beliefs and professional values needs to consider how to reconcile these. Here I will report some of the ways that social workers have used to manage this type of conflict. These strategies are clearly not equally acceptable, yet there may be differences of opinions on what is and what is not acceptable. Every social worker will have to consider carefully which of these ways (or perhaps some other way) he or she can follow in good conscience.

• Those who want to be social workers must give up or waive their religious beliefs whenever these are in conflict with professional values. Thus Levy, who chaired the NASW committee that drafted the professional code of ethics, wrote: "To be a professional practitioner is to give up some of one's autonomy and to relinquish some of one's right as a freely functioning human being" (1976a:113). A person who wants to be a social worker has voluntarily accepted a series of special obligations. At times these special obligations take priority and limit that person's right to choose other values, such as religious values, as behavioral guides (Fishkin 1982). "The social worker's professional ethics must transcend his personal ethics when the two are not entirely reconcilable" (Levy 1976b:112). If the social work ideology calls for supporting the client's decision, Darlene Porter's social worker must support her request for an abortion, no matter what his or her own religious values may say in this matter.

• Another way of coping with this conflict is for the social worker to differentiate between the professional techniques he or she employs and the theology he or she believes in. This will permit grounding the philosophical outlook in a religiously instructed faith stance, even while working professionally as a practical positivist. But the price for this approach may be "a schizophrenic view of reality" (Sneck and Bonica 1980:35). However, many have noted that this approach is in line with the reality that religion in modern society has become a segmented activity with relatively little relevance for the concerns of daily life. A religious social worker who follow this approach will support Darlene's request for an abortion, just as did the colleague who utilized the first option discussed above. The difference between them is that this second social worker acknowledges that his or her own personal religious values are not relevant to professional practice decisions. The first social worker, on the other hand, may believe that even though religious values are relevant in this case, the professional values take precedence over the personal values.

• Some social workers withdraw from conflict situations in order not to compromise their own values. There are several different withdrawal techniques that have been used. One is to become so busy elsewhere that one does not even realize that a conflict exists. By being busy with other clients, the social worker can delay meeting with Darlene. Or attention can be concentrated on one of Darlene's other problems that may be identified as more urgent than her abortion request. Perhaps the most common and most responsible withdrawal strategy is to refer the conflict-causing situation or client to another social worker whose religious values do not preclude dealing with the specific request.

• The conflict can be avoided or reduced by defining social work values in terms of one's religious values. "Help becomes in a new sense the expression of one's religion, not just as the term is often used, one's general but unspecific good will toward men, but what one actually believes in" (Keith-Lucas 1972:205–6). Professional values will be defined so that they are identical with one's religious values. Believing social workers may not even be aware that they face a conflict or a dilemma because they consider their religious beliefs as eternal and overriding all other temporal ideologies. Affairs of this world are of secondary importance. The principal task in this world is to prepare for eternal life. This obligation applies to social workers, as it does to all persons. If religious law prohibits abortions under these or any circumstances, a religious social worker would help Darlene to accept her pregnancy and avoid an abortion. It is the worker's "professional" obligation to help Darlene get ready for eternal life. Many social workers do not think that this is an acceptable strategy.

• Other alternatives include anger, guilt, or blaming the client. These options are not really helpful because they neither resolve the conflict nor help the worker find direction for helping Darlene Porter.

The discontinuity or clash between religious and professional values may be more severe a problem for Christians than for the adherents of other faiths. For Jewish social workers, for example, the conflict will be much less acute because Jews have traditionally based their religious beliefs, doctrines, and practices on an evolving oral tradition rather than on the written text of the Bible. Thus Nahmanides (1194–1270), one of the foremost Jewish medieval Bible commentators, summarily dismissed the literal account of the Creation story. This widely accepted interpretation helped many believing Jews to avoid or moderate the science/religion conflict that has occupied the attention of so many modern Christian theologians. Similarly, the disciples of many Oriental religions do not seem to understand the kind of conflicts I have discussed in the last few pages because their religious beliefs are (in our language) much less dogmatic and much more pragmatic.

Whenever one's own values differ from those of one's associates, a shift of values toward those of the colleague group is likely. This is particularly apt to happen when the original set of values does not seem entirely relevant for the new situation. Blau and Scott (1962) presented many research findings that support the strength of the reference group. In their study, professional social workers abandoned professional values and accepted the bureaucratic ideology of their nonprofessional colleagues, while in other settings nonprofessionals accepted those professional values that were dominant among their colleagues. Social workers may relax their religious beliefs when they work together with colleagues committed to a secular social work ideology. This may occur especially when working in a secular, nonsectarian agency.

Some religious authorities see this magnetic attraction of the reference group as a danger that may weaken attachment to religious values and religious institutions. This is one reason (but not the only one) for establishing social work programs in denominational colleges, for continuing sectarian agencies, and for promoting separate sectarian professional organizations for social workers who belong to a given denomination or church. The magnitude of the conflict will, of course, be greatly reduced in those sectarian agencies that fully support religious values. But most American social workers, including many religiously committed practitioners, will continue to work in public agencies and other nonsectarian settings where, at least potentially, they may face a conflict between their religious and their professional values.

Chapter Five

Practice Issues and Dilemmas

Religious considerations are usually not the primary focus in the social work interaction, but there are few situations in which they are entirely absent. For some clients (and for some social workers) religion may be more important than for others; in some problem situations religious considerations may be closer to the surface than in others—but rarely if ever can religious considerations be ignored altogether.

In this chapter we will consider various problems, issues, and dilemmas that social workers face. All involve some aspect of religion. Some of these are particularly cogent when working with religiously oriented clients, others are more relevant when the client comes from a secular background. All deserve the serious consideration of social workers who want to deliver effective services.

The professional demand for sensitivity and empathy is discussed in the first section of this chapter. This is not a "religious" issue, but a basic requirement in the professional helping process. The discussion here will focus on the dilemma of social workers (secular as well as religious) who face clients with life-styles and religious practices that are, for the social workers, completely strange and incomprehensible. The impact of religious beliefs, practices, and observances on the social work process is examined in this connection. Can these be used constructively to help clients help themselves or are these practices to be viewed as interferences?

Some have advocated the use of prayer as a helping resource, while others have raised questions about this. I will examine the use of prayer in the social work process. Next, I take note of the possible connection between religiosity and psychopathology. I will review some of the studies that have presented evidence for and against this causal hypothesis. In analyzing this material I draw attention to the difference between neurotic and healthy religion, and raise the question of whether a social worker should ever help a client abandon maladaptive religious behaviors.

Social workers are ethically committed to practice "in the best interest of the client." However, there may not always be agreement on what is "best" for a given client. Particular problems may arise around the issue of spiritual benefits and spiritual harm. The discussion will review ways in which a social worker can take these elements into consideration.

The concepts of sin and guilt have all but disappeared from the professional vocabulary, yet for many clients these are issue that are close to the surface or at the center of their problem. My analysis begins with a reconsideration of the idea of responsibility in human behavior and leads to an examination of sin and guilt in the social work practice context.

Many clients, not only those who are religiously oriented, tend to focus excessively on themselves, on their problems, weaknesses, and limitations, to the exclusion of other healthier parts of their personalities. "Dereflection" is a social work skill that can be helpful with such clients. However, I will point to potential problems encountered in the use of this technique.

A problem that religious social workers face at times is what to do when a client requests the worker's help to do something that the worker believes to be illicit, such as having an abortion. Various ways of coping with this type of dilemma are considered.

It is a mistake to conclude from the foregoing that this chapter is limited to a consideration of problems faced only by religious people. In various ways these problems are also faced by clients and workers who appear to be far removed from any religious influence. A dramatic example of how religion impacts on the problem of a completely secular client suggests that there are religious aspects in working with almost every client. The issues and dilemmas discussed in this chapter should therefore receive the serious attention of all social workers.

Sensitivity and Empathy

It is generally agreed that a high degree of sensitivity for a client's problems and for the way he or she views the world is an indispensable element of the helping process. Most social workers are sensitive persons. They have accepted as "a fundamental tenet of practice wisdom that empathy is an essential ingredient in the professional helping process" and that it is "one of the critical variables affecting the outcome of the helping process" (Keefe 1976:10).

Although sensitivity and empathy are important attributes for social workers, they are not sufficient to guarantee successful goal achievement (Macarov 1978; Mitchell, Bozarth, and Krauft 1977). Nevertheless, a sensitive understanding of the other's world seems desirable, even if we accept Skinner's pithy comment that "two people cannot suffer each other's toothaches, recall each other's memories, or share each other's happiness" (1964:83). Carkhuff summed up the professional consensus when he wrote, "Without an empathetic understanding of the helpee's world and his difficulties as he sees them there is no basis for helping" (1969:173).

Yet there is one area where this empathetic understanding and sensitivity is often wanting. Frequently social workers report that religion simply is not important for their clients and that therefore their clients do not talk about it. This may be so—or it may be that these social workers are not ready to listen to what some of their clients have to say because they themselves disvalue the importance of religion and religious values. These social workers may have accepted the view that religion is no more than "a leisure-time activity." They will cite as evidence reports that there is no essential difference between church members and the unchurched (Berger 1961:38, 4). For them, as for so many others in the contemporary world, religion has become an amorphous force that is of little importance.

It is no wonder that as a result of such views some social workers fail to pay sufficient sympathetic attention to their clients' religious values, beliefs, and practices. The problem is that for some of their clients religion is important, perhaps *the* most important factor in their lives, while for many social workers religion is completely unimportant. This gap can lead to serious consequences. Siporin and Glasser have expressed concern about "this discrepancy [which] is growing wider because of the burgeoning religious revival taking place in this country, a revival that seems much more influential among the general population than among helping professionals" (1987:24).

The above comments apply especially when clients are devoutly religious persons. For them, all values and all orientations derive their importance from their idea of God, even when their concept of God is fuzzy or not completely conscious. Their moral life, their philosophy of life, their outlook on life as a whole—all of these are derived from their concept of God (Nilsen 1980). The sensitive social worker who inquires into such clients' concerns about religion will elicit an enormous amount of relevant material. Not to do so with religiously active clients means closing the door to one of the most crucial parts of their lives.

Religion: Key for Diagnosis

Many claim that religion also makes a difference among those not so strongly committed to religion, especially at times of crisis. Since the request for professional help often comes as a result of a crisis experience, it may be appropriate to take the spiritual and religious aspects of every client's life experiences into consideration.

Frankl warned that those who "ignore man's spiritual side [are] giving away one of his most valuable assets" (1968:x). A social worker's understanding of every client's problem will be enriched by a careful and sensitive regard for the person's moral and spiritual convictions. This important practice principle has been neglected for too long by too many social workers (Goldstein 1986). This neglect is especially strange in view of the fact that even Freud, who thought of religion as a form of mass neurosis, recognized it as a key for understanding his patients' social and human consciousness (Wilson 1982:4). Frankl also wrote that "the proper diagnosis can be made only by someone who can see the spiritual side of man" (1968:ix). In many instances religion is not only the key to a proper diagnosis of the problem, but also a crucial resource for helping clients solve their problems. Religion can be a source of strength for those clients who are believers. By including the religious and spiritual elements, the social worker can facilitate these clients' attempts to rebuild their lives.

Many social workers accept the general principle of sensitivity and empathetic understanding of a client's religious values, beliefs, and practices, but encounter difficulties when they want to apply this principle in practice. Two brief examples will illustrate this practice problem.

GLOSSOLALIA

Glossolalia or "speaking in tongues" in a nonunderstandable language under the inspiration of the Holy Spirit is a phenomenon encountered among the members of a number of Christian denominations and sects. This behavior, which is highly valued by the members of these groups, has been described by outsiders variously as "anomalous," "aberrant," or "extraordinary" (Malony and Lovekin 1985). A social worker, even a religiously committed social worker, who is not a glossolalist may find it difficult to relate to a client who "speaks in tongues" since such behavior is completely foreign to his or her own way of life. But sensitive understanding does not require that the social worker accept the client's way of life or beliefs; instead it asks that the social worker try to understand the client on the client's terms of reference.

Glossolalia may be a search for a more immediate religious experience, it may be a form of mysticism, or it may mean still something else to the client. It is important to give every client an opportunity to explain what this behavior means to him or her, how it fits into his or her world, and what questions it raises. Social workers know how to encourage client verbal participation: structuring, focusing, timing, setting the tone, and providing verbal feedback are some of the crucial worker skills that facilitate client communication and can be used to help these clients (Loewenberg 1983:237–58).

WOMEN'S ROLES

Many women with a deep religious commitment have found it difficult to reconcile their role and status in society with the position adopted by their church. There is no one view on the role of women to which all churches subscribe. Differences range from complete equality (including ordination to the ministry, full and active participation in worship and governance, equal religious obligations and responsibilities, etc.) to complete subordination in all religious spheres. Generally speaking, liberal churches have tended to maintain an egalitarian position, while fundamentalist and orthodox religious groups have tended to oppose it.

Some scholars have attempted to show that fundamentalist religion relegates women to a place of inferiority, subordination, and even subservience to males (Hurley 1981). But others have found flaws in this interpretation and have noted that both men and women have been the recipients of spiritual gifts (Bilezikian 1985). Christenson, an influential evangelist, has argued for women's equality and for their submission at one and the same time: "The wife is fully equal to the husband, as Christ is equal to God; yet she remains submissive to her husband in all things, as the Son is submissive to his Father" (1977:22). Many social workers find it difficult to accept such a position, while others may identify completely with it. Admittedly, it is not for social workers to determine which is the "correct" theological position. However, they may face a practice dilemma when one of their clients comes from a religious environment that is not egalitarian.

A social worker who cannot accept anything but a fully egalitarian position will not find it easy to help a client who has a role/status problem but who prefers to cope with this problem without leaving her church. Similarly, another social worker who has a deep commitment to the teachings of a church that assigns distinct roles to men and women will not find it easy to work with a client who prefers to resolve her role or status problem by leaving the church or by attempting to introduce radical innovations into the church. Both types of social workers need to remember that it is their function to help troubled clients to resolve their problems, even when the outcome may not be exactly what the worker prefers.

One of the most important steps in this helping process is sensitive and sympathetic listening. But beyond this, empathy also requires knowledge and understanding. All social workers, and especially all those who are comfortable with their own views on the issue of religious egalitarianism, need to understand better the views, feelings, and problems of women in fundamentalist or orthodox churches. Superficial comparisons to other discriminated minority groups may not be overly helpful and may disguise a wealth of important information.

Few social workers deny the importance of sensitivity and empathy. But at times these worker characteristics are missing when it comes to the area of religion. This may be the result of an undervaluation of the significance of religion in clients' lives or it may be the result of too wide a gap between the client's and worker's values. Empathy in professional relations does not require that the practitioner accept the client's values, but it does call for a sensitive and knowledgeable understanding of the client's value position.

Religious Beliefs and Rituals

Some have suggested that religious beliefs and practices should never become the focus of the social work helping process because these are things that can neither be proven nor disproven in any objective way (Bowers 1969). But social workers who approach people as whole persons cannot randomly select the focus of attention nor can they arbitrarily exclude experiences that are of central importance to their clients. However, social workers should be cautious lest they select for attention isolated religious beliefs or rituals without taking into consideration the total picture. An example may clarify these problems.

Case 5.1: A Case of Compulsive Hand Washing

Ed Crane, age twenty-two, married and the father of three young children, has been unable to hold a regular job. You are his social worker and have just been assigned to this case. However, he has been known to the agency for a number of years. From the case record you learn that Ed was raised in a very traditional family that has actively participated in a small fundamentalist church ever since Ed was a child. Ed is now an elder in this church. The previous social workers wrote that Ed takes his religion very seriously.

In you first meeting with Ed he told you that the reason he cannot hold a regular job is because of the many religious practices that he must perform throughout the day. When asked for an example of a practice that interfered with his holding a job, he mentioned that he must wash his hands whenever he touches any part of his body, even his face. Every time this happens (and it happens quite often), he must stop whatever he is doing, find a sink, wash his hands, and recite the appropriate prayers.

Some social workers will treat this hand-washing ritual as a manifestation of a compulsive behavior, without considering at all the religious aspects of this ritualistic behavior. Others will recognize that religion is a central element in Ed's life; these social workers may focus on the hand washing as a dysfunctional religious ritual, without taking into consideration the total situation. The hand washing may be symptomatic of a psychopathology or of a genuine religious experience.

It will be of some importance for correct problem assessment to learn if this behavior is a part of the religious ritual practiced by all members of this church, or perhaps only by those who have a very strong identification with the beliefs of the group—or whether this is an idiosyncratic ritual developed by Ed alone. The effective social worker needs to inquire about the religious validity of what appears to be excessive hand washing. This information will help in arriving at a more accurate diagnosis. However, even if the worker discovers that Ed's church does not require this ritual observance, it will be difficult to convince Ed to abandon this mistaken practice.

Trying to counsel a client to change a behavior that is strongly anchored in important values, such as religious values, is rarely successful (even when the basis for such a ritual is in error). But some social workers believe that they have a responsibility to attempt to introduce changes in cases like Ed's since these behaviors are damaging not only for the client but also for other family members. Often people like Ed use religious terminology to defend their life-style or to hide their pathology.

It may be tempting for a social worker to try to convince such clients that their interpretation of religious requirements are in error. Ed's social worker could have questioned how other members of his church manage to keep on working. Perhaps the requirement is not as rigid as Ed made it appear. But such a logical, objective approach may lead to a trap. Since the basis for observing a religious ritual is almost never a logical one, it is doubtful whether any amount of logical arguments will persuade Ed to reassess his religious observances. On the other hand, it may be possible to help people like Ed consider two or more relevant religious images or metaphors simultaneously. This, according to Stovich, may "break through the rigid holding patterns and pave the way for more movement" (1985:121).

Some religiously committed clients may use their religious

beliefs as a defense mechanism to avoid full participation in the helping encounter. Such persons may try to stop further discussion of their problem by suddenly announcing that this problem is a spiritual one. Ed Crane, in a later session, was discussing the problematic relationship between his wife and himself. But whenever the social worker tried to lead the conversation from generalities to specifics, Ed would refuse to continue, claiming that his religion forbade talking about sexual matters. Even the social worker who knows that this is a misuse of religious law must respect the client's wish not to discuss the particular matter. Perhaps consultation with religious authorities may suggest a way to permit persons like Ed to participate more fully in the helping process while at the same time observing their religious law.

RITUALS AND OBSERVANCES

For many people religious beliefs and practices serve positive functions in maintaining their mental health. Even though the family that prays together will not always stay together, family religious rituals do create a bond and a sense of belonging that have helped many to survive the stress and strain of daily life. People in crisis situations often turn to religious ritual for comfort, guidance, and relief. Even those social workers who do not acknowledge the efficacy of sacraments should recognize that for believers they have deep meaning and can make significant differences. Making arrangements for a religiously committed house-bound older adult to attend a religious service or to receive Holy Communion may be more helpful than almost anything else a social worker can do for such a person. Whether or not providing this help is really helpful will depend, of course, on an accurate assessment of the client and his or her total situation.

There are ritualistic behaviors and religious observances that many social workers will consider quite strange. For example, religious experiences such as "hearing voices" are considered real by the members of many cultural groups, but are thought to be pathological in the cultural groups from which many social workers come. One study reported that a majority of Mexican-American high school students considered "voices" a real religious experience, while 90 percent of white Anglo psychiatric residents identified such experiences as psychopathological (Flax et al. 1979). The mourning observances practiced by Orthodox Jews may seem morbid to a social worker who was raised in a culture that tries to avoid everything connected with death. The attention paid to dietary laws by observant Muslims and Jews may seem excessive to those who think of eating purely as a physiological activity. But what may seem pathological to some practitioners may be conducive to positive mental health in the context in which it is normative. The effective social worker will want to encourage, not discourage, such religious activities since they may help clients strengthen their identification with their own group and thereby raise their self-image.

The rigid rules that require the observance of minute rituals may seem meaningless or even pathogenic to many social workers, but these may have real meaning to the religious client. Research findings report that participation in fundamentalist religious activity can lead to a reduction of emotional distress (Ness and Wintrob 1980). Immersion in the religious activities of a cult can help individuals become stronger, find greater self-fulfillment, and experience greater self-control (Gordon 1984; Galanter 1982; but see Delgado 1980 and Levine 1980 for findings of pathological consequences resulting from cult participation). This does not mean that participation in religious activities is always therapeutic or beneficial. But the mere fact that a person prays five times a day does not necessarily mean that she or he is compulsive or mentally ill.

RELIGIOUS RITUAL AS A RESOURCE

Tomko (1985) described her use of religious ritual in her work with immobile hospital patients. Since she recognized the psychological and emotional benefits that can be derived from religious experiences, she arranged for various religious rituals to be conducted in the hospital, even though she had to overcome considerable administrative obstacles before she could do so. In one instance she arranged a "parallel" funeral service for a deceased husband in the hospital room where his wife was hospitalized. In another case this social worker arranged for an infant's baptism in the hospital room of his mother who was about to die of cancer. In these instances, as well as in many others, this social worker used social work practice skills to effect goal achievement. The religious ritual was not viewed as an end in itself but rather as an available resource.

PRAYER

It has been suggested that prayer is an appropriate strategy when working with religious clients. Caplis (1983) asked social workers not to overlook the possible therapeutic values of prayer. Some religious social workers have utilized prayer as an intervention technique because they believe in prayer's efficacy. Secular social workers may see other reasons for using prayer. Researchers at the Thorndike Memorial Laboratories of Harvard University have reported that various relaxation techniques may lead to the same results; a phrase, a sound, a prayer, or a mantra may be sufficient to shift the mind from the stressful, externally oriented world to a more passive attitude which is an essential element in relaxation. Benson (1985) noted that if relaxation is the goal, there is no clinical reason for not using prayers with which the client is comfortable. Though Meystedt (1984) was not entirely certain that prayer was just as effective as other relaxation techniques, he also agreed that its use was proper, and with certain clients was perhaps the best available technique. "Although it does not quite reach the reduction level of relaxation training, it appears to be an effective and credible solution for those clients who are religiously oriented" (Meystedt 1984:223).

A number of Christian therapists have presented strong arguments for using prayer to help their clients. Sanford (1977), a Jungian analyst and Episcopalian priest, placed great emphasis on the importance of prayer for persons who seek psychological help and growth experiences. He urged his patients to pray in whatever way is natural for them. Calabrese and Proctor (1976) pray for and with their clients because they consider prayer to be at the heart of the therapeutic process. Similarly, Tyrrell (1982), an analyst and Catholic priest, emphasized the centrality of prayer in the helping process. Through prayer "God's power is invited directly into situations of pain, injustice or disorder" (Gatza 1979). Judah (1985), on the other hand, cautioned that prayer should not become part of the therapeutic relationship; without discouraging prayer, she thought it best that clients pray in their own churches and not in the social worker's office.

Prayer fills a variety of different functions in various religions. Social workers must learn to recognize these if they want to be effective helpers. Existentialist religion stresses the I/Thou communication aspect of prayer. Other belief systems accept prayer and pilgrimages to holy places as methods for obtaining relief for physical and spiritual problems. Some religions caution the faithful not to expect direct answers to their prayers. Whatever the role assigned to prayer, when clients believe in the efficacy of prayer, they should not be discouraged from engaging in it.

However, no one has suggested that prayer is a social worker's panacea. Prayer may be an important avenue of help for some clients; it may provide relief and relaxation in stressful situations, but rarely will prayer alone correct a problem situation. Nevertheless, it is important to recognize that prayer may permit some clients to mobilize themselves sufficiently to begin to do something about their situation.

Religiosity and Psychopathology

Bergin (1983), on the basis of an analysis of twenty-four studies on the relationship between religiosity and personality, found no support for the view that religious belief or activity is necessarily correlated with psychopathology. Spero (1985) distinguished between neurotic and healthy religiosity. He suggested that unhealthy religion reflects the disordered use to which conflicted persons put religion, rather than a basic pathology of religion itself. He identified a number of indicators of such unhealthy or disordered religion, including the following:

> 1. The current intensity of religiosity or level of religious practice is of relatively recent origin and has caused a break with one or more significant others (family, friends, work group, etc.).
> 2. This person's history has been characterized by a number of religious "crises," by numerous changes in church affiliation, and/or by frequent changes in the level or intensity of religious observances.
> 3. The person, afraid of "backsliding," has adopted an interpretation of religious requirements that is more rigid than that followed by most persons affiliated with the same religious group.
> 4. This person continues to be unhappy and immobile following a religious conversion (based on Spero 1985:20–21).

Some have suggested that it is not religiosity that leads to pathology, but rather that psychopathology distorts or impedes religious practices (Bechhofer 1983, Stark 1971). At times people who are already disturbed co-opt religiosity into the service of their pathology, but this should not be taken to mean that all ritualistic behavior is pathogenic. Yet it may happen that ritualistic behaviors do support existing pathological conditions. Peteet (1981) wondered whether there are situations in which a social worker would be justified to undermine a client's religious faith. What should a social worker do when it is clear that religious practices and beliefs support maladaptive behaviors?

Under these circumstances there are some who approve of a professional intervention designed to help a client to abandon neurotic religious behaviors and beliefs (London 1976), but others do not approve and call instead for extreme caution (McLemore and Court 1977). Spero (1980) urged that practitioners help disturbed clients to experience religion in a healthier way, but he stopped short of supporting practitioner activities designed to undermine a client's faith. However, many social workers will not be able to help others experience religion in a healthy way since they themselves never experienced religion in this manner. Consultation with religious authorities may be helpful in these situations.

Religiosity and Mental Health

While a great deal of effort has been directed toward establishing the connection between religiosity and pathology, not enough attention has been paid to the connection between religiosity and mental health. This imbalance should be redressed. Many have noted the importance of communal rituals, both religious and civic, for affirming the societal moral order, as well as for reestablishing group and community cohesion. On an individual level such rituals tend to provide reinforcement for more effective social functioning and more skillful coping in difficult situations. Religious rituals and ceremonies, as well as religious faith and values, are important assets for individual and family development and functioning. "Such assets also tend to strengthen individual and group esteem, morale, and cohesion in the face of stress and crisis," according to Siporin (1985a:17).

Spiritual Harm

A difficult practice dilemma occurs when a social worker can provide the best possible service only by disregarding the religious beliefs of the client. In theory, no social worker would want to do this, but real practice situations at times place the social worker before hard choices. I will illustrate this kind of practice dilemma by considering the problem that faced Tom's social worker.

Case 5.2: Tom Needs a Placement

Tom is a young child who cannot stay in his own home for the next few months (and perhaps for a longer period). Tom's parents have requested that he be placed with a family whose religious beliefs and practices are like theirs.

The agency has had poor experiences with the only foster home that meets the request of Tom's parents. The social worker feels that a placement with this family will be a harmful experience for Tom. She knows, however, that there is a possibility to place Tom with a warm, receptive family where he will have a good experience, but this family is not affiliated with any church and does not observe any religious rituals.

Or, consider the dilemma that faced David Kirk's social worker:

Case 5.3: Refusing a Job

David Kirk, married and the father of four young children, has been out of work for several months. His social worker finally located a job opening that appeared suitable, but this job requires working on Saturdays. Mr. Kirk is a strict Sabbath observer and refused to take this job.

What is a worker's role in these and similar situations? What is in the best interest of these clients? David Kirk is an adult who can make his own decision about working or not working on the Sabbath, but what about Tom, who is too young to decide which foster home is better for him? Because Tom comes from a religious environment, most social workers would give some consideration to the religious factor. But is it ethical for a professional practitioner to agree to an "unsuitable" placement if Tom's parents insist on a foster family that is affiliated with their church, and this "unsuitable" home is the only one available that meets the parents' specification?

In considering these questions, the social worker must keep in mind that different people define "harm" in quite different ways. These differences will influence practice decisions, since the prevention of harm is both a basic human need and a high-priority professional criterion. For example, David Kirk may be convinced that breaking the Commandments by working on the Sabbath is more detrimental than remaining unemployed. Tom's parents may prefer the unsuitable home to the spiritual damage that would be caused by placing their son in an agnostic home. Some social workers, on the other hand, will attach greater weight to the psychological harm that may be caused by long-term unemployment or the physical harm that may result from placement in an unsuitable home. Social workers have an obligation to raise these questions so that clients can take these factors into consideration when making their decisions. But in the final analysis, the decision is that of the client. Only in cases where serious physical or psychological danger is imminent should the social worker turn to the courts for a determination that may override the client's wish.

A similar dilemma faces the hospital social worker who deals with families whose religious beliefs preclude traditional medical treatment. While a physician must ultimately decide whether there is medical urgency that requires application to the courts for an order that permits medical treatment despite the family's objection, social workers can provide several important services that may help to resolve the problem situation amicably and more quickly. They can serve as a two-way information channel, providing the family with an accurate risk assessment and offering the medical staff a clearer picture of this family's specific objections. Having this information, the physician can suggest an alternate procedure to which the family might agree. On the other hand, once members of the family are aware of the precise risks involved in withholding treatment, they might want to consult with their own religious authority to determine what is permissible under the specific circumstances (Rockowitz, Korpela, and Hunter 1981).

Responsibility, Sin, and Guilt

There are belief systems that portray the human being as weak and entirely dependent on God and his mercy. Other belief systems teach that humans are strong and that they can act autonomously. Still others suggest that both of these views describe the condition of modern individuals—they are at the same time both weak and strong, dependent and autonomous. Do these various views make any difference for social work practice?

There is no room for social work or for any other type of human intervention in a belief system that is entirely deterministic, where a person's fate is determined entirely by God or by some other external force, where there is no free will and no freedom of choice, because the assumption of responsibility for one's fate and for what one does is a basic precondition for every human change effort. However, as I pointed out earlier, there are few belief systems that completely discount human efforts. They may allow for more or for less autonomous activity. They may demand more or less dependence on God or upon religious leaders. But almost never does religious commitment require complete passivity or total subservience. Indeed, in many cases religion has been the force that has freed people and has given them the opportunity for greater choice and more activity (Frankl 1968:59).

PERSONAL RESPONSIBILITY IN SOCIAL WORK

Note should be taken that one ideological position in contemporary social work all but rejects the notion of personal responsibility. By locating the cause of all social problems in malfunctions or faults of the societal system (such as social injustice, discrimination, exploitation, etc.) those following this approach in effect relieve individuals of all (or almost all) responsibility for their current situation. No more than a person can be held responsible for an appendicitis attack can he or she be held responsible for being unemployed or for being an alcoholic. These social workers will concentrate most of their efforts on societal changes since they believe that individual changes without societal changes are not feasible.

Many other social workers say that the cause of problems may indeed be a societal fault or it may be the result of an individual malfunction, or, most often, it may be the result of a combination of both. These social workers refuse to assume a priori where the problem source is located. For these social workers, personal responsibility is a very real possibility. Still other social workers say that the question of problem causation is not crucial. No matter where or what the cause for the current situation, the important question is how the person reacts to the problem situation that he or she now faces. While an individual may not be "responsible" for the problem, he or she is accountable for the response to the current predicament. Some cope more adequately than others. In seemingly identical situations, some continue their lives with a great deal of optimism and with real attempts to solve their problems, while others fall apart or engage in coping mechanisms that are neither appropriate nor effective. Every person must take responsibility for his or her actions—responsibility not in terms guilt, but in terms of accepting the possibility that he or she can do something about their response to the current situation. This kind of client response will facilitate the efficacy of social work intervention.

"Responsibility" can become a two-edged sword when working with some religiously committed clients. Though responsibility for one's actions is an essential condition for change, some clients have established for themselves goals of perfection that are not attainable by any human being. They may base this goal on a literal interpretation of Matthew's admonition (5.48): "You therefore must be perfect, as your heavenly Father is perfect." They do not realize that complete perfection is a divine attribute toward which humans always strive but which they never achieve. A more realistic approach may be the one presented in Philippians 3.12: "Not that I have already obtained this or am already perfect; but I press on to make it my own. . . . " Those who want to achieve nothing less than complete perfection assume responsibility for events over which they have often very little control.

Failure to reach such an unrealistic goal may lead to depression, despondency, and even suicidal ideas (Stern 1985:39). Social workers who work with such clients should be aware that the source of the problem is not something that the client has or has not done in the past, but rather the use of inappropriate or unrealistic assessment criteria. One way to help in situations of this kind is to assist these clients to recast the concept of "complete perfection" from the past to the future so that it becomes a goal to be approached instead of an assessment criterion for past or current behavior.

SIN AND GUILT

Closely related to the concept of responsibility is that of sin and guilt. Even though the term "sin" has just about disappeared from the American public vocabulary, it continues to occupy the attention of many. Sin has been variously defined as a transgression of the divine law, as disobedience of God's will, or as failure to realize the moral ideal in one's behavior. Psychiatrist Menninger defined sin in the following way: "The wrongness of the sinful act lies not merely in . . . its departure from the accepted, appropriate way of behavior, but in an implicitly aggressive quality—a ruthlessness, a hurting, a breaking away from God and from the rest of humanity, a partial alienation or act of rebellion" (1973:19).

A subtle change has occurred in the way in which people view the concept of sin. Since the close of the Middle Ages the state has defined as criminal many acts that previously the church had considered sinful. The conversion of many sins into crimes has made the remaining sins increasingly private and intimate. This privatization became even stronger when the Protestant churches abolished the ritual of confession. From a mental health point of view, this shift from external social controls to internal self-control has increased the psychological burdens of many people to the point where they can no longer function without external help.

This is a particularly severe problem for Christians, since in many versions of Christian theology everybody is considered as innately sinful and guilty, frail and unable to escape from sin through one's own efforts. This view of the human being contrasts sharply with that of many other belief systems. For example, the concept of sin is virtually unknown in Buddhism and plays only an insignificant role in Shintoism. It is present in Judaism, but occupies an entirely different role since it is within every person's capacity to reverse the sinful behavior and earn divine forgiveness. But since the clients of most American social workers are Christians or are influenced by Christian value systems, further consideration of sin and of the associated concepts of guilt and forgiveness are necessary.

Sin implies guilt and guilt presupposes individual responsibility. In the Freudian version, guilt is defined as ego anxiety over punishment or loss of love from the superego. In *Civilization and Its Discontents* (1946) Freud distinguished between real and neurotic guilt. Though in many of his writings he seemed to emphasize only the latter, this distinction is of some significance. Real guilt results from some problematic behavior in which the person has engaged, while neurotic guilt is an irrational guilt that arises out of an imagined transgression or a situation for which, viewed objectively, the person carried no responsibility. An example of neurotic guilt is the guilt a person feels for the death of a parent or a child when there was nothing that person could have done to prevent the death from happening. This type of guilt is quite different from the guilt that arises from a client's engaging in an extramarital affair, a behavior pattern that the client initiated and that he or she can reverse. Bergin wrote, "In the one case, we are dealing with a victim and, in the other, with a perpetrator. In one case, guilt needs to be reduced and, in the other, it needs to become prominent so as to cause the perpetrator to change those actions that are harmful to others" (1982).

An example of the kind of irrational guilt seen by many social workers occurs when parents of children born with a serious birth defect believe that they are being punished for some sin they had committed many years earlier. When these social workers attempt to assess the extent of ego damage suffered by such parents, they should try to identify the source of the guilt feelings—whether they are based on valid religious concepts, on irrational fears, or on regression to childhood fears. Social workers should not engage in guilt reduction attempts before they are certain that there is no objective cause for the guilt. They must remember that the social worker–client relationship is essentially a utilitarian one and not a sacred one. "Its aim . . . is healing, not salvation" (Kung 1979). The social worker's task is not to grant absolution or to alleviate guilt feelings at any cost, but to help the client function in more effective ways. If the guilt is real, the client should be helped to transform the guilt-producing behavior into a more moral and a more satisfying behavior. If, on the other hand, the guilt is neurotic, the client must be helped to understand the irrational basis for his feelings.

In the face of guilt, the single most important helping activity, according to Tyrrell (1982), is *acceptance* of the guilt-ridden person. Those who feel guilty, no matter whether their guilt is real or neurotic, cannot accept themselves. This does not mean that social workers necessarily must condone problematic behaviors, but it does mean that they should accept the client as a person, just as he or she is. This acceptance constitutes a crucial first step in helping such people toward more effective functioning.

Dereflection

Many who are concerned with their guilt turn for help to a social worker. If the client is a religious person, this concern may also be expressed in religious terms. Clients who have sinned will want to change, confess, do penance, or undertake the appropriate rituals. For them, sin is not a figment of their imagination, but a crucial part of the world that requires change. In these situations, the social worker must remember that it is not a professional function to hear the confession or to indicate the appropriate penance. These specific tasks belong to the priest, minister, rabbi, or elder. But the ritual is only one step in problem solving. These clients must also acquire relevant coping behaviors. This is the phase of problem solving that is certainly within the domain of social work. One of the ways of helping these clients is to redirect the focus of their attention away from themselves, away from their anxieties, and away from the source of their problem and instead help them focus on their strengths and on the intact parts of their personality. Frankl (1963) called this technique *dereflection*.

At the same time social workers must understand that a focus on the self is not always undesirable. As a matter of fact, coming to terms with the self is a prerequisite for resolving intrapersonal concerns. It is the *exclusive* focus on self that is dysfunctional and perhaps even damaging. This may be what Buber had in mind when he wrote that "human beings should begin with themselves [but] they should not end with themselves" (1965:11). Preoccupation with self is often a cause for concern and in certain situations requires professional intervention. Dereflection is the skill used by a social worker who attempts to expand the client's horizon from an exclusive focus on self to a wider perspective.

Religion and the Secular Client

For many people today religion is meaningless. Those who grew up in a religious home and left the church as adolescents or adults may still not have resolved the struggle that led to the break. But an increasing number of people are the children, grandchildren, and even great-grandchildren of people who themselves had never had any contact with formal religion. It may be argued that for these people religion may indeed not be a relevant force and that much of what we have examined in the previous chapters may not apply. However, Frankl was of the opinion that men and women are "often much more religious than [they] suspect" (1968:xx).

Those who define religion as "a set of symbolic forms and acts which relate man to the ultimate condition of his existence" (Bellah 1964:358) will, of course, find that people, even secular people, will be more religious than even they themselves suspect because everyone must relate to the ultimate questions of life and death. However, Frankl's observation may apply even when we define religion more narrowly, as I have done throughout this volume. The following case illustration, taken from the practice of Jung (1961:139–40), supports this proposition.

Jung once described his therapeutic work with a secular patient. In this therapeutic relationship religion proved to be the focal point, even though neither Jung nor the patient would have thought so in the beginning stages of the therapy. The patient was a young, analyzed, secularized, enlightened Jewish woman who requested therapy to relieve the symptoms of a severe anxiety neurosis. Jung learned in the course of treatment that the woman's grandfather was a well-known Hassidic rabbi whose followers considered him to be a *zaddik* (a charismatic religious leader, wonder healer, and miracle worker, who employs his mystical powers within and on behalf of the community of his followers, and who at the same time serves as confessor, moral instructor, and practical adviser for his followers). Her father had rejected this religious tradition completely, viewing it as utter nonsense. This tradition also had no meaning or relevance for the young woman who was Jung's patient. Jung felt nevertheless that it was related to her present condition. He told her, "Now I am going to tell you something you may not be able to accept. Your grandfather was a *zaddik*. . . . Your father betrayed the secret and turned his back to God. And you have your neurosis because the fear of God has gotten into you." Jung continued his report by writing that his words struck the young lady "like a bolt of lightning." Within a week this patient was "cured."

Jung's patient was a completely secular person who had never had any contact with formal religion; it appeared that religion was a subject that was completely irrelevant for her. In this respect she resembled many of the clients whom social workers see daily. Nevertheless, a religious struggle proved to be a core aspect of the problem of Jung's patient. I have reported this case at some length to point out that religious elements may be involved in some problem situations that at first glance seem far removed from religion. I am not suggesting that Jung's style serve as a model for social workers who face similar problems. A social worker would certainly approach this case in a different way. Nor am I suggesting that religion will prove to be the core element in every or even in most problems brought to a social worker. But I am saying that social workers should not exclude automatically from consideration any aspect of religion just because the client comes from a secular background.

Cooperation Dilemma

Special dilemmas may arise when a secular client receives service from a religiously motivated practitioner. At times such a client may ask his or her social worker to do something that the social worker believes is prohibited by his or her faith, but that the client does not consider forbidden. Catholic moral theologians refer to this as the problem of cooperation, that is, the moral questions that arise when one person is asked to help another person perform an act that the first person believes to be wrong. This dilemma is not limited to Catholic social workers but has been experienced by many religiously committed social workers of all faiths. Though these situations may not arise frequently, when they do occur thy create a difficult problem for the religious social worker. This problem arises most typically in situations where the secular society has legalized or approved an activity that religious law prohibits or disapproves of. One example of this problem in social work practice involves requests for abortions or sterilizations, but these are not the only practice areas where a cooperation dilemma can occur.

This problem involves a conflict between two rights—the right of the client to request a service that society permits and the right of the social worker to follow the dictates of his or her conscience and not cooperate in an act that he or she considers to be wrong. Thus, Darlene Porter (case 4.2) requested an abortion; as far as she was concerned, there is nothing wrong with having an abortion. Contemporary American society and the courts support a woman's right to have an abortion. However, the religious social worker who received Darlene's request may face a dilemma if he or she believes that to cooperate in obtaining an abortion is an "immoral" act. Given this situation, the social worker may respond in a number of different ways when asked to "cooperate."

REFUSAL

The social worker who receives this request can refuse to offer the service, explaining to Ms. Porter that he or she does not offer this service. The worker may or may not explain the reasons for this refusal. Refusing the request raises the problem of equity: a client is entitled to receive the same services, no matter to which social worker she has been assigned. If the religious social worker refuses to cooperate, Ms. Porter will not receive the same service that other social workers in the same agency would have offered. But by refusing, this worker has avoided facing the dilemma of cooperation.

PERSUASION

Counseling is a recognized professional function. Every social worker, no matter what his or her values, will want to explore with Ms. Porter the various alternatives that are open to her before she makes a final decision. Without access to full information, her initial request for an abortion may not meet the requirements for full and informed consent (Loewenberg and Dolgoff 1985:57–64). In the counseling process the worker may unintentionally stress one option more than another. Or the worker may consciously use this opportunity to persuade the client to agree to an option that the worker thinks is best for the client or that is most desirable from a societal point of view. A worker who disapproves of abortions may present other alternatives in a much more positive way than would a colleague who does not disapprove. Or this worker may stress the possible dangers of abortions, without discussing the dangers inherent in other options. When it comes to persuasion, there is a thin line between what is ethical and what is not. While some types of persuasion are permissible, departing from the truth or misleading a client by not presenting all available information is not an ethical professional behavior.

AVOIDANCE

A social worker can try to avoid becoming involved in situations where the worker's religious beliefs counterindicate offering a service which a client requests. The worker may be so "busy" that there is no time to discuss the request. Or the worker may focus attention on another problem that the client has and that does not involve the need to consider the request for an "illicit" service.

Some have suggested that social workers who have this problem should avoid accepting jobs that might involve them in the dilemma of cooperation. Thus one writer urged that a social worker should not counsel women with unwanted pregnancies if her beliefs "make it impossible for her to allow her clients to choose any of the alternatives, [including] abortion or adoption or keeping and raising the child" (Potts 1971:270). This advice may fit the "specialist" social worker, but a religious social worker in general practice can hardly avoid receiving this type of request.

REFERRAL

A social worker whose beliefs make it impossible to offer a service that a client has requested legitimately can refer this client to a colleague who is willing to provide this service. An official NASW publication suggested that "if a social worker chooses not to participate in abortion counseling, it is his or her responsibility to provide appropriate referral services to assure that this option is available to clients" (NASW 1978:4). When a social worker's religious principles make it impossible for him or her to respond to Darlene Porter's request (case 4.2) for help in arranging an abortion, the worker may refer the client to another social worker who is willing to deal with this request. However, some may consider that the act of referring a client to another social worker is also a form of cooperation that may violate their religious beliefs. They ask whether there is any moral difference between referring a client to an abortion clinic, where a physician will decide whether and how to perform the abortion, and referring the client to another social worker who has no qualms about referring the client to an abortion clinic.

REDEFINING COOPERATION

Timms (1983) argued for a revision of the cooperation concept on the basis of the widespread acceptance of religious freedom and toleration of differences in contemporary society. A social worker may believe that abortion is morally wrong, but the client does not share this assessment. In fact, a client like Darlene Porter may define abortion as desirable and morally good. This social worker should be able to help Darlene obtain an abortion without cooperating with the client's bad will because this client has no bad will (Curran 1975). It is characteristic of the contemporary world that we are in contact daily with people of whose behavior we do not approve. By "cooperating" the social worker is not saying that this behavior is morally correct. "Without unduly sacrificing his own conscientious principles" the social worker who faces such a problem can reason that he or she is providing a service to which the client has a right (Timms 1983:43).

SEGREGATION

Many religiously committed social workers avoid the cooperation dilemma by segregating their religious beliefs from their practice activities. In this case, the person who goes to church on Sunday is not the same person who makes professional decisions on Monday. "What the church has said to him might conceivably have bearing on his private life. But it is quite irrelevant to his involvement in public (and professional) life" (Berger 1961:37). When the Catholic church excommunicated the executive director of a Planned Parenthood clinic, she insisted that her religious faith remained unshaken but on "human-rights issues . . . many of us Catholics consider ourselves in conflict with the church" (Sorrentino 1986:20). Transplanting the "separation of church and state" principle from the public to the personal sphere permits individuals to believe one thing in their own personal lives, but to practice according to a different value set in their professional roles.

Religious social workers who have faced the cooperation dilemma are familiar with one or more of these "solutions." Arguments can be presented for and against each of them, suggesting that there is no one perfect solution. It is not uncommon for the same social worker to utilize different options when dealing with different problem situations, taking into consideration such factors as imminent danger to the client and others, reversibility, and the clarity of religious guidelines. Some workers have sought religious guidance in coping with dilemmas of this type, while others will attempt to reach a decision by themselves. The secular supervisor of such workers does not face problems of this nature, but should be aware of the difficult spiritual conflict that the worker may be facing.

Chapter Six

Social Work and Religious Organizations

There are various practice issues and dilemmas that commonly arise when social workers work with or in religious organizations or with members of the clergy. The church and the clergy are viewed as community resources that may, if correctly utilized, serve as important participants in the social work action system. Since most Americans have more contact with a religious organization than with a social service agency, the former can become an important source of support. This is particularly true in the case of religiously oriented clients.

Effective relations with the clergy should consist of reciprocal interactions. Clergy persons may refer people with problems to social agencies. Since churches are located in the neighborhood community, they often serve as a first address when a person faces a crisis. Their skillful handling and accurate preliminary assessment may make an important contribution to the eventual outcome of the social work intervention process.

But referral must work both ways. At times social workers will want to use the expertise of clergy persons, either for consultation around specific questions with religious implications or for the referral of clients who would be better served by a direct contact with a clergy person. The conditions governing such referrals and the cautions that should be observed will be examined.

Much of social work practice was and still is carried out under sectarian auspices. The various types of social agencies under religious auspices will be examined, as will be the question of whether and to what extent such sponsorship affects service delivery patterns. Special attention will be paid to such critical areas as restricted staffing, client eligibility policies, budget problems, and so on.

Churches as Community Resources

For many people the church and the clergy are crucial community resources which are involved (implicitly or explicitly) in every area of life. The responses of Americans to a large-scale study about mental health services indicate that when facing a personal problem, many more requested help from the clergy than from a social agency. Forty-two percent of the respondents indicated that they had sought "professional help for a personal problem" from their clergyman, while only 16 percent had turned to a social agency, a social worker, or a marriage counselor (Gurin, Veroff, and Feld 1960). Most Americans have an ongoing, even if weak and sporadic contact with a church, while they do not have such a continuing relationship with a social agency. Even among those who do turn for help to a social worker, there are many who also have a long-standing relationship with a church. This church may play an important part, even an essential part, in their lives. Seven out of every ten adult Americans reported that they were members of a church or synagogue, while four out of every ten actually attended a church service during a typical week (Gallup 1985). For all of these adults, the church or the synagogue is a significant resource in the community.

No social worker has suggested that religious experiences are a panacea for every problem or for every person, but there is increasing recognition that for believers religion is a resource that should not be overlooked. This has been recognized by social workers who themselves are religiously committed, as well as by those who do not believe.

Churches and Religious Groups as Support Systems

Social workers' utilization of religious groups as support systems is still uneven. For some it comes only as an afterthought, while other social workers use these as a central element in their action system. An example of the latter approach is Joseph and Patrick's (1980) parish neighborhood model, which is not a revised model of the traditional sectarian social agency, but represents an imaginative use of a community development model in a parish setting. In this model, the local parish provides not only space for and access to social service programs, but perhaps even more important, it provides opportunities for involving strangers and isolated people in community networks. The parish renewal program, sponsored by the bishops, is a parallel effort which can extend the coverage of service. In 1982, 53 of 120 dioceses surveyed had a parish social ministry program (NCCC 1983b).

Another example of the use of this resource occurs when a religious community is used as the family in the treatment of priests, monks, and nuns. This model was described by social workers who practice family therapy and who have conceptualized the religious community as the family unit of reference. Without the active involvement of both the family and the religious community, the treatment process was said to be limited (Jones et al. 1985).

There are those who see positive functions in all types of religious groupings, no matter how much they depart from traditional forms. Sects, because they are usually small and because they emphasize the direct person-to-person relationship, can serve as powerful support and reference groups. This holds true whether we think of the Mormon's stake and ward organization, the Jehovah's Witnesses Bible study group, or the *hoza* system of the Rissho-Kosei-Kai. Though theologically these three faith groups are light years apart, from a sociological and psychological viewpoint they fill similar functions. But this function is met only for those who are fully committed to the sect or cult and to its teachings. While some have pointed to the psychological risks that cult membership may entail, there are others who do not share this assessment. Joining an esoteric cult need not necessarily be viewed as a sign of psychopathology, but can be an essentially healthy way of coping with stress (Pattison 1980). Other benefical effects of cult membership have been reported by Stones (1978), Galanter (1980, 1982), and Galanter and Buckley (1978).

Gordon (1984), a participant observer in two Jesus People groups, reported that the "abandonment to the group" helped members to become stronger, find greater self-fulfillment, and gain greater self-control. Other studies have focused on the dysfunctional aspects of cult membership, especially on the brainwashing-like indoctrination process that new recruits must undergo. Delgado (1980) and Levine (1980) reported on the pathological personality changes that resulted from cult membership. Kaslow and Sussman (1982) presented a comprehensive collection of essays reflecting all sides of the debate on cults. Mental health professionals, including social workers, are not of one mind in their assessment of the esoteric cults that have sprung up all over the Western world. But there is little doubt that the growing interest in non-Western religions does suggest that for some they offer meaning and support that had not been found in more traditional religious groups.

The growth of Pentacostal membership among the immigrants from traditionally Catholic Puerto Rico has been attributed to the recent arrivals' attempt to cope with the anomie and stress resulting from the migration experience. For these immigrants, as well as for so many others who have found it difficult to adjust to the stresses and strains of modern urban life, religious affiliation represents an attempt "to redevelop the community in the new urban situation" (Poblete and O'Dea 1960). The sect-type religious group, with its emphasis on personal fellowship, may be better suited to fill this function than the more impersonal church-type congregation.

Support groups and other informal groupings have also appeared within many of the more formal church-type religious organizations. Networks whose members provide each other with moral support appear as Bible study groups, religious discussion groups, informal groups that celebrate religious occasions together, and so forth. Often these networks attempt to return to an earlier style of worship; always they try to add face-to-face contact to the more formal religious ceremonies. These groups may be part of the charismatic movement or they will emphasize equal participation instead of hierarchical distinctions. Each in its way attempts to introduce the benefits of the sect to some of the members of a church-type religious organization.

Role of The Clergy

Caplan and Killilea (1976) observed that most mental health professionals, including social workers, see their clients or patients at most only a few hours each week. But if therapy is to be effective (or if an additional crisis is to be avoided), there is the need for constant and ongoing support and reinforcement, at least for a period of time. This support and reinforcement can be provided only by the family and the community. Religious leaders should be included as natural community helpers. They should be recruited into the community helping system.

Establishing working relationships with other professionals in the community, whether they be clergy, physician, police, teacher, or other, is never easy. There are always questions of "turf," as well as problems of communication, ranging from the use of jargon to considerations of confidentiality. While progress has been made in establishing working relationships with various professional groups, many social workers have not yet found satisfactory ways of working together with the clergy.

One of the reasons for failing to use the clergy as a community resource is that many social workers have found it difficult to bring about the positive and effective involvement of the clergy in the social work action system. A great deal of creative thought on the part of both social workers and the church will be required to achieve a measure of positive cooperation. Clarification of the respective roles of clergy and social work is a crucial first step if the collaboration of these two groups is to be of value to the client-member (Boverman 1969).

REFERRAL AND CONSULTATION

Many social workers will refer a client to a clergy person whenever a religious problem or question arises, but this may not always be the best way of helping. Even though a social worker is not a religious authority and should not decide religious questions for others, the fact that there are religious elements in a problem situation does not necessarily mean that a social worker cannot render effective help. Before referring a client to a clergy person, a social worker should examine the reasons for the referral. Is the referral in the best interest of the client? Or are there other reasons for choosing this strategy? The following are some of the situations in which one must exercise cautious consideration before making a referral to a member of the clergy:

1. Is the social worker reluctant to deal with religious and value-laden problems?

2. Is the social worker more concerned that the client remain faithful to the church doctrines than in helping the client resolve his or her problem?

3. Does the social worker want to transfer a very difficult or "impossible" problem to someone else so that his or her "success" rate remains unblemished?

When the answer to any of these questions is positive, the social worker is likely to refer a problem that really should be his or her responsibility.

Referring a client to the "religious problem specialist" may also be counterindicated when a client has chosen to bring the problem in the first place to a social worker and not to a clergy person because he or she was too embarrassed or too ashamed to seek help from that person for this particular problem (Spero 1985).

Instead of referring the client to the clergy, it may be more effective for the social worker to seek consultation with a clergy person in order to clarify thoughts on a problem situation that involves religious issues (Weiss 1982). Consultation may be indicated whenever a social worker suspects that a religious belief or practice is pathogenic. Such consultation will help the social worker to understand better whether the client has co-opted religion to aggravate a psychological disturbance. It may also indicate ways in which the social worker can help this client to experience religion in a healthier way. Consultation, finally, will prevent referring a disturbed person to a religious leader who is apt to reinforce the pathology (Bowers 1969).

Some social workers are disturbed by the fact that there are members of the clergy who undertake even the most highly professionalized social work functions, such as family counseling and individual therapy. They are ambivalent about the continuing growth of training programs in pastoral counseling because such programs suggest that these are legitimate activities for the clergy. The reality, however, is that the "clergy will remain in roles paralleling those of social workers" (Reid and Stimpson 1987:552). Rather than suspect the motives of the clergy, social workers should consider and encourage the possible role of ministers and priests as gatekeepers to the mental health system (Rumberger and Rogers 1982).

The Sectarian Agency

During the past century many churches and church groups initiated a large variety of social services and welfare institutions. These included city rescue missions, YMCAs, YWCAs, and other charitable and philanthropic organizations (Olmstead 1970:142–44). In time, some of these services dropped their church affiliations and became secular, community-sponsored, non sectarian social agencies, while others retained their church affiliations. The reasons for establishing and maintaining religious social agencies have varied; they include the following:

1. Social service is viewed as the contemporary way of bringing the message of religion to the people.

2. The church has sought to develop a variety of services in order to retain the interest and loyalty of those members who feel less of a need for the traditional religious and spiritual services.

3. People may feel more at ease when they ask for help from a social agency whose workers share their religious identification and values. Ethnic minority groups, especially those who still prefer to speak in their native language, appreciate sectarian agencies that provide workers who speak their own language and identify with their ethnic heritage.

4. A religious social agency will take into consideration the special needs arising out of religious obligations and life-styles of church members.

5. By providing social services within a religious framework there will be fewer temptations for church members to cast aside their religious obligations.

6. There may be financial advantages for the church that sponsors a social agency. Bequests from private donors and grants from government that ordinarily would not flow to churches may become available in this way.

Though these reasons are not exclusive and more than one may figure in the decision to sponsor a social agency, one or the other reason usually dominates or is decisive.

SOCIAL WORK UNDER RELIGIOUS AUSPICES

Information on the amount of social work carried out by sectarian organizations is "at best, fragmentary, and, at worst, misleading"

(Reid 1977:1247). In 1966 there were reported to be 955 sectarian residential institutions in the United States; 545 of these were institutions for dependent and neglected children. Just over 60,000 children were in sectarian institutions, while almost twice that number, or 104,000, were found in nonsectarian or public institutions (Reid 1977). A somewhat different picture emerges from a 1982 survey of NASW members; at that time, 8.78 percent of the employed respondents reported that they practiced under sectarian auspices (NASW 1985, table B).

The most current *Encyclopedia of Social Work* does not present any statistical data or estimates on the extent of social work services sponsored by sectarian agencies (Reid and Stimpson 1987). Although the data on the number and type of sectarian agencies or social workers in these agencies is far from certain, there is no doubt that an important part of social services is delivered by organizations under religious auspices.

Many different types of social agencies are classified as "religious" or "sectarian," but not all sectarian agencies are "religious." One way to classify sectarian agencies is by their relationship or linkage to the sponsoring church organization. If we do this, we will obtain the following typology:

Church-sponsored agencies: these social agencies are sponsored by a local church, a regional church body, a denomination, or by the religious hierarchy. The Salvation Army Social Service Center is an example of this type. The Catholic Social Services are another example, even though the linkage of the local agency is generally to the diocese. The church has full legal and spiritual authority and control over this type of social agency.

The autonomous Institution: this social agency is an independent body but is in close contact with a church. Despite its structural and legal independence, it considers itself under the "spiritual jurisdiction" of a church or a religious leader. Yet this type of sectarian agency is separate from the church's administrative structure. For example, most Lutheran multiservice social agencies are legally separate bodies and not part of the church that "sponsors" them. The Lutheran Church Missouri Synod has specifically stated that it will not be responsible for any debts incurred by its related social agencies and welfare institutions. Even so, the Lutheran Social Service System requires that affiliated agencies integrate "Christian theology" into their professional program and practice (Reid and Stimpson 1987:553).

Agencies sponsored by an ethnic community: the social agency is sponsored or operated by an ethnic community that is popularly identified with a religious group or is coexistent with a religious group. Thus, most Jewish social agencies are not sponsored by or related to a synagogue, but are sponsored by the secular Jewish community.

In what ways, if any, does the religious sponsorship or affiliation of a social agency impact on social work practice? There may be as many different answers to this question as there are sectarian social agencies. The influence may be minor and nonsubstantial—or it may be major, to the point where it may be difficult to identify staff activities as professional social work. Whenever the clientele and/or the staff are selected according to religious affiliation criteria, the usual social work criteria have become less prominent. It does not matter whether this "selection" occurred as a result of a specific agency policy (for example, when the intake is limited to members of a certain denomination) or as the result of client self-selection (generally only Catholics turn to Catholic Charities, even though this agency "welcomes the participation of those of other faiths and, indeed, of all persons of good will" (NCCC 1983a:17)). This does not necessarily mean that the quality of the services rendered is less professional, but it does introduce a difference—a difference that, generally speaking, supports the rationale for establishing and maintaining the sectarian agency.

Restrictive Policies. There may be times, however, when agency policy restricts practice. Restrictions that hamper practice are not limited to religious agencies, but may and do occur in all types of agencies. When the city welfare department closes a shelter for battered wives because of budgetary restrictions, social workers can no longer make use of this resource and must turn to others, perhaps less adequate ones. When a social agency instructs its social workers to place children in a particular home because this institution is sponsored by the church, it makes it virtually impossible for these social workers to consider other alternatives that may be better suited for a particular child. When agency policy precludes abortions as an intervention strategy, it limits the strategies available to social workers employed by that agency. Whether the reason for a policy is budgetary or religious or a reflection of public policy is almost immaterial in its effect on social work practice. Social workers who disagree with a restrictive policy and who see it as a threat to professional practice must decide how to respond—whether to refuse to work under these circumstances, to attempt to initiate a change process, to circumvent the policy, or to accept it for the time being.

However, the situation is different when the restrictive policy is based on religious values and the social workers concerned accept these values. These workers will not interpret the policy as limiting their autonomy and will not attempt to change it or circumvent it. Instead they will welcome the policy because it supports the religious values in which they believe. Whenever the worker's and the agency's religious orientations are identical, special care must be taken to protect the rights of clients, especially the rights of clients who do not share this religious orientation.

Staffing. Staffing patterns of sectarian social agencies range from those that employ only certified church members to those that have an open hiring policy and use employment criteria that do not include the applicant's religious affiliation. In most sectarian agencies most workers identify with the beliefs of the sponsoring denomination. But sectarian agencies that as a matter of policy employ only members of their own denomination are believed to be in the minority. This may be so because few agencies can afford to forego government funds, which often make up as much as half of the agency budget. All agencies, even sectarian agencies, that are accredited through the Council on Accreditation of Services for Families and Children must present a clear statement of affirmative action and must hire personnel without any discrimination, not even discrimination on religious grounds. A number of the larger religious organizations, including the National Conference of Catholic Charities, the Lutheran Social Service System, and the Association of Jewish Family and Children's Agencies, belong to this Council on Accreditation (Reid and Stimpson 1987:551–52).

A Buddhist social worker can be found in a Jewish home for the aged, and a Baptist social worker in a Catholic Charities office. A social service agency, however, may decide to give employment preference to social workers who are members of the church or denomination with which it is affiliated because it believes in the importance of shared values, goals, and norms. While ordinarily organization socialization will influence such a commitment toward church doctrines, when too many staff members hold different, noncongruent values, this commitment may become weakened and may in time disappear. Hiring policies will depend in large measure on the major reason for establishing and maintaining the agency as a sectarian organization. Aside from budgetary considerations, these policies will reflect the sponsoring group's priority, whether it is to place a greater emphasis on the professional quality of the social work services, or on staff compliance with religious doctrines and beliefs. Whenever the qualifications of candidates for a vacant position are not strong on both the professional and the religious criteria, the decision whether to give more weight to one or to the other factor will be crucial. In time, the agency's decision in this matter becomes known and candidates who do not meet the agency's preference will no longer present themselves. When it becomes widely known that a certain agency invariably gives preference to candidates who are members in good standing of a certain denomination or church, social workers who do not belong usually will not apply—even though this agency on a formal basis subscribes to a policy of nondiscrimination.

Client Eligibility. The "selection" of a clientele is one of the most crucial decisions that every organization faces. While changes in this area are possible, this is not the kind of decision that is modified frequently. A social agency must frame this decision in terms of defining who is eligible to receive services. This eligibility decision is closely related to the major reason for operating the agency. For a sectarian agency client eligibility may range from an "open" policy where an applicant's religion is not a relevant criterion to a "closed" policy where services are provided only to members of the church or denomination that sponsors the agency.

Eligibility policy and actual practice do not always coincide. An agency may have an open eligibility policy, but in fact attract only clients from one denomination. There may be a historical reason for this or it may be a question of geography. An agency that is located in a religiously homogeneous neighborhood generally will have a clientele that reflects this population composition, no matter what the agency's formal policy. The receipt of federal funds or funds from a Community Chest may be tied to a requirement for "open eligibility." Nevertheless, the vast majority of clients in most sectarian social agencies tend to identify with the sponsoring religious group (Reid and Stimpson 1987:551).

WORKING TOGETHER: SECTARIAN AND
NONSECTARIAN AGENCIES
In most American communities there are many social agencies; some are sectarian and others nonsectarian. In what ways, if any, can or should these agencies work together? It has been suggested that the ideal type of relationship is one of partnership, but this may be an oversimplistic notion which tends to conceal some of the difficulties that occur in real life. A more realistic model should reflect the plurality of values that exist in a community. This plurality also characterizes the social welfare sector.

Most sectarian agencies participate in the work of the community-wide United Way or a similar community welfare planning council. Often these agencies take leadership positions in these community-wide organizations. On a more immediate and operational level, most sectarian agencies cooperate with other sectarian and nonsectarian agencies on specific projects or in relation to specific clients. But a merger of different agencies is not always the most cost-effective plan, even though this might seem like a good idea. The availability of a number of different agencies with different value emphases may result in broader community support for social welfare programs generally. What is needed is not a merger, not even a formalized partnership, but a creative and cooperative coexistence where no one agency feels threatened by the success of another.

CRITICAL QUESTIONS
The sharpest attacks on the continued existence of sectarian social agencies have come from within the religious community. For example, a generation ago, Donald Howard wrote to the director of the Department of Social Welfare of the National Council of Churches of Christ suggesting that churches focus the attention of their work on meeting the spiritual needs of their members and not to spend their

limited resources on needs that others can meet (personal communication, cited by Coughlin 1965:23). At first glance, this advice is reminiscent of the views of the fundamentalist preachers cited in chapter 1. But there is a crucial difference between the two positions. While Billy Sunday attacked social work as evil, Howard, who himself was once a dean of a graduate school of social work, supports social work but questions the church's involvement in a service that he believes is rendered better and more effectively by social workers in professional social work agencies.

Howard's advice evidently was not heeded. Church-sponsored social agencies and institutions continue to function. Some provide superior services; others are mismanaged. In 1977, Pacific Homes, a Methodist-affiliated retirement home, went bankrupt. Residents who had paid large sums of money for lifetime service sued the Methodist church. An out-of-court settlement for $21 million was reached after lengthy litigation. These legal proceedings and the settlement were said to have diverted millions of dollars from church programs and missions. They devoured months of church staff time and drained the energy and morale of many who really had wanted to devote themselves to church work. As a consequence of the Pacific Homes case, the Methodist church tightened its practices with respect to the social service agencies and institutions that it sponsors (Netting 1984). Other churches have done the same. But I do not know of any church that has divested itself of social services as a result of the Pacific Homes case.

INNOVATIONS

One of the advantages claimed for sectarian agencies is that they, like all voluntary organizations, have the freedom to innovate new program ideas and to organize populations at risk, even when this displeases the powerful establishment. However, both the development of innovative programs and the sponsorship of community action programs requires a relatively large and secure resource base, a requirement that many church agencies do not meet. In the last decade or so, sectarian agencies have come to depend increasingly on government funds. By 1982 government funding constituted approximately half of their income. Federal budget cuts in recent years have resulted in severe deficits and recurring crises in sectarian as well as in nonsectarian agencies. While some of these agencies have developed new strategies that stress "creativity and revitalization," many have had to restrict their traditional programs and limit drastically any thoughts about innovations.

One church-sponsored agency that evidently does not have such problems is the New Life Evangelistic Center in Saint Louis. Like many other religious organizations, NLEC provides a variety of social and community services for the poor and the homeless. It differs from most other organizations in that poor people control the organization, make all decisions, and fill most paid jobs. Professional positions are staffed by volunteers. The most crucial difference is that the organization generates enough income to cover a four-million-dollar annual budget without any need to depend on government support. Its assets include both a radio and a television station. With such a secure financial base, the agency's programs are little affected by federal decisions to cut welfare budgets.

Part III

Epilogue

Chapter Seven

Agenda for Today and Tomorrow

As American society prepares itself for the final decade of the twentieth century, it is clear that religion is an issue that cannot be ignored. While evidence concerning the extent of the religious revival is uneven and perhaps contradictory, few doubt that religion continues to occupy a significant and vital role in the daily life of large groups in the population. Religiously committed clients and social workers are not an anachronism left over from another era, but a living reality. This being the case, social workers (no matter what their own beliefs) must not close their eyes to the possible impact of religion. Practitioners, both those who believe as well as those who do not, must learn to understand religion and its impact on human behavior. Such understanding is a prerequisite for effective practice.

When working with religions clients, social work practice calls for sympathetic consideration of their beliefs. More than that, religious institutions, rituals, and practices can become significant resources which should not be overlooked when working with clients for whom these are important. But sensitivity and empathy, important as they are, are not sufficient. These worker characteristics must be backed up by knowledge.

There is urgent need for empirical research to strengthen the social work knowledge base generally. Research is no less necessary when it comes to knowledge about the religious aspects of social work practice. The research questions in this area that require investigation are many. They include the following:

• Does differentiating between "judging a person" and "judging his or her behavior" make for more effective social work practice? (This question is of special relevance to many religiously oriented social workers who cannot help but judge a person's behavior.)

• Does matching clients and social workers according to their religious values make for more effective social work practice?

• Does it make for more effective social work practice when a social worker informs the client of his or her religious stance?

• Do social workers whose approach to practice tends to be more deterministic emphasize social change methods, while those with a stronger commitment to individual autonomy and free will favor the casework methodology? (Faculty members, especially those in religiously sponsored social work education programs, will want to take any findings on this question into consideration when planning or redesigning the curriculum.)

These questions are illustrative only. Many others beg to be asked. Obviously, much work still needs to be done to develop efficient research designs that will permit answering these and other questions.

The production of new knowledge through empirical research will be valuable only to the extent that this new knowledge can be used by practitioners. It is important, therefore, that the researchers bear in mind that the objective is not knowledge for its own sake, but knowledge that will permit practitioners to provide more effective services. Social work educators have three responsibilities in this matter. They must produce new knowledge, they must train new researchers, and they must teach students how to use the new knowledge in their practice.

But the issue of religion in social work practice goes beyond the production and introduction of new empirical knowledge. Social work practitioners should also be able to generate insights and information from their daily practice in order to help to further specify the role of the religious factor in social work practice. In addition, there exists an already large body of knowledge that is not fully used. We must pay closer attention to the broad area of values because generally values are relevant to the religious factor. This area of values is all too often ignored or considered only marginally, both in academia and in the field.

In order to insure that new workers enter the field with a strong social work practice base, it is important that material that deals with religious values and religious practices be included in the social work curriculum. Students should be helped to explore these values and rituals so that they can better assess their implications for social work practice. Practitioners already in the field also need to be helped to relate more constructively to this material through the use of workshops and in-service training courses.

Kane (1986) wrote that to make decisions about how care should be organized to meet human needs and to determine what should be the goal and role of a profession like social work, we must utilize the "tools of philosophy and moral theory." Such a view will require a much more intensive consideration of religion and the religious factor in social work practice then has been customary until now.

America is becoming a more pluralistic society than it ever was before. The large number of immigrants arriving from Latin America and the Far East will result in a radically different population, a fact that will soon be reflected in the case loads of many social workers. There will be changes in color, language, life-style, values, religion, and the type of problems that these new clients will bring to the social agency. This new situation will not be without problems, but social workers who have a long tradition of acceptance and tolerance will know how to rise to this new challenge, as they have risen successfully to earlier challenges of this sort.

Bibliography

Abramson, Marcia and Rita Beck Black. 1985. "Extending the Boundaries of Life: Implications for Practice." *Health and Social Work* 10(3):165–73.

Acock, Alan C. and Theodore Fuller. 1984. "The Attitude-Behavior Relationship and Parental Influence: Circular Mobility in Thailand." *Social Forces* 62:973–94.

Adler, Zsuzsanna and James Midgley. 1978. "Social Work Education in Developing Countries." *Social Work Today* 9(48):16–17.

Allport, Gordon W. 1950. *The Individual and His Religion*. New York: Macmillan.

—— 1966. "The Religious Context of Prejudice." *Journal for the Scientific Study of Religion* 5:447–57.

Allport, Gordon W. and Michael Ross. 1967. "Personal Religious Orientation and Prejudice." *Journal of Personality and Social Psychology* 5:432–43.

Aschenbrenner, Karl. 1971. *The Concept of Value: Foundations of Value Theory*. Dordrecht, Holland: Reidel.

Barker-Benfield, G. J. 1976. "A Historical Perspective on Women's Health Care." *Women and Health* 1:13–15.

Barry, Brian M. 1973. *A Liberal Theory of Justice*. Oxford: Clarendon Press.

Bartlett, Harriet M. 1970. *The Common Base of Social Work Practice*. New York: National Association of Social Workers.

Baum, Naomi, Haya Izhaki, Meir Loewenberg, and David Portowitz. 1987. "The Impact of Religious Beliefs on Social Work Practice." *Social Work and Social Policy in Israel* 1(1).

Bechhofer, Richard. 1983. "Judaism and Counseling: Perspectives and Comparisons." Baltimore: Johns Hopkins University, Division of Education. ERIC Document ED 237 826.

Beit-Hallahmi, Benjamin. 1975. "Encountering Orthodox Religions in Psychotherapy." *Psychotherapy* 12:357–59.

Bellah, Robert N. 1964. "Religious Evolution." *American Sociological Review* 29:358–74.

Bellah, Robert N. et al. 1985. *Habits of the Heart: Individualism and Commitment in American Life*. Berkeley: University of California Press.

Bellah, Robert N. and Phillip E. Hammond. 1980. *Varieties of Civil Religions.* New York: Harper and Row.

Bem, D. J. 1970. *Beliefs, Attitudes, and Human Affairs.* Belmont, Calif.: Brooks/Cole.

Benson, Herbert. 1985. "The Relaxation Response." In A. Monat and R. S. Lazarus, eds., *Stress and Coping,* pp. 315–21. 2d ed. New York: Columbia University Press.

Berger, Peter L. 1961. *The Noise of Solemn Assemblies.* New York: Doubleday.

—— 1977. *Facing Up to Modernity.* New York: Penguin Books.

Bergin, Allen E. 1980. "Psychotherapy and Religious Values." *Journal of Consulting and Clinical Psychology* 48:95–105.

—— 1982. "The Search for a Psychotherapy of Value." *Tijdschrift voor Psychotherapie* (Amsterdam), vol. 7.

—— 1983. "Religiosity and Mental Health: A Critical Reevaluation and Meta-Analysis." *Professional Psychology* 14:170–84.

Bibby, Reginald W. 1983. "The Moral Mosaic: Sexuality in the Canadian 80s." *Social Indicators Research* 13:171–84.

Biestek, Felix P. 1953. "The Non-Judgmental Attitude." *Social Casework* 34(6):235–39.

Bilezikian, Gilbert. 1985. *Beyond Sex Roles: A Guide for the Study of Female Roles in the Bible.* Grand Rapids, Mich.: Baker Book.

Bisno, Herbert. 1952. *The Philosophy of Social Work.* Washington, D.C.: Public Affairs Press.

Blau, Peter M. and Richard W. Scott. 1962. *Formal Organizations.* San Francisco: Chandler.

Bloom, Martin. 1975. *The Paradox of Helping: Introduction to the Philosophy of Scientific Helping.* New York: Wiley.

Boverman, M. 1969. "Psychiatrist-Clergy Collaboration in Psychotherapy." In E. M. Pattison, ed., *Clinical Psychiatry and Religion,* pp. 279–91. Boston: Little, Brown.

Bowers, M. K. 1969. "Psychotherapy of Religious Conflict." In E. M. Pattison, ed., *Clinical Psychiatry and Religion,* pp. 233–42. Boston: Little, Brown.

Box, S. and S. Cotgrove. 1966. "Scientific Identity, Occupational Selection, and Role Strain." *British Journal of Sociology* 17:20–28.

Brown, Bertram S. 1968. "Social Change: A Professional Challenge." Typescript.

Buber, Martin, 1965. *Between Man and Man.* Translated by Ronald G. Smith. New York: Macmillan.

Bucher, R. and A. Strauss. 1961. "Professions in Process." *American Journal of Sociology* 66:325–34.

Cain, Lillian P. 1979. "Social Workers' Role in Teen-Age Abortion." *Social Work* 24:52–56.

Calabrese, Alphonso and William Proctor. 1976. *The Christian Love Treatment.* Garden City, N. Y.: Doubleday.

Caplan, Gerald and M. Killilea, eds. 1976. *Support Systems and Mutual Help.* New York: Grune and Stratton.

Caplis, Regina. 1983. "Catholic Social Service and Transcendental Values." *Social Thought* 9(1):3–16.

Caplow, Theodore. 1983. *All Faithful People*. Minneapolis: University of Minnesota Press.

Caplow, Theodore et al. 1982. *Middletown Families*. Minneapolis: University of Minnesota Press.

Carkhuff, R. F. 1969. *Helping and Human Relations*. New York: Holt, Rinehart, and Winston.

Christenson, L. 1977. "Families Need a Head." *Viewpoints: Christian Perspectives on Social Concerns: The Family in Crisis*. Minneapolis, Minn.: Augsburg, pp. 21–24.

Clebsch, William D. 1968. *From Sacred to Profane America*. New York: Harper and Row.

Coll, Blanche D. 1969. *Perspectives in Public Welfare: A History*. Washington: U.S. Department of Health, Education and Welfare.

Compton, Beulah and Burt Galaway. 1979. *Social Work Processes*. Rev. ed. New York: Dorsey.

Cooney, Timothy J. 1985. *Telling Right from Wrong*. Buffalo, N. Y.: Prometheus.

Coser, Lewis. 1956. *The Functions of Social Conflict*. New York: Free Press.

Coughlin, Bernard F. 1965. *Church and State in Social Welfare*. New York: Columbia University Press.

Council on Social Work Education (CSWE). 1982. *Curriculum Policy Statement*. New York: CSWE.

Cross, Darryl G. and Janet A. Khan. 1983. "The Values of Three Practitioner Groups: Religious and Moral Aspects." *Counseling and Values* 28(1):13–19.

Cox, Harvey. 1984. *Religion in the Secular City: Toward a Post-Modern Theology*. New York: Simon and Schuster.

Cuddihy, John M. 1978. *No Offense: Civil Religion and Protestant Taste*. New York: Seabury.

Curnock, Kathleen and Pauline Hardiker. 1979. *Towards Practice Theory: Skills and Methods in Social Assessment*. London: Routledge and Kegan Paul.

Curran, Charles E. 1975. "Cooperation: Toward a Revision of the Concept and Its Application." *Catholic Medical Quarterly* 26(5):194–209.

Daner, Francine J. 1974. *The American Children of KRSNA*. New York: Holt, Rinehart and Winston.

D'Antonio, William V. and Steven Stact. 1980. "Religion, Family Size, and Abortion: Extending Renzi's Hypothesis." *Journal for the Scientific Study of Religion* 19:397–409.

Davis, Kingsley. 1948. *Human Society*. New York: Macmillan.

DeFelicia, Judith. 1982. "The Impact of Professional Social Work Education Upon the Acceptance of the Practice Principle 'Don't Impose Your Own Personal Values on the Client.' " DSW dissertation, Adelphi University, Garden City, N.Y.

Delgado, Richard. 1980. "Limits to Proselytizing." *Society* 17:25–33.

Deregando, Baron. 1832. *Visitors of the Poor*. Translated by a Lady of Boston.

DeSchweinitz, Karl. 1972(1943). *England's Road to Social Security.* New York: Barnes.

De Tocqueville, Alexis. 1954(1835). *Democracy in America.* 2 vols. P. Bradley, ed. New York: Vintage Books.

Dewey, John. 1922. *Human Nature and Conduct.* New York: Random House.

—— 1929. *The Quest for Certainty.* New York: Putnam, Capricorn Books.

Durkheim, Emile. 1954(1912). *The Elementary Forms of the Religious Life.* J. W. Swain, tr. New York: Free Press.

Eckardt, Ralph W. Jr. 1974. "Evangelical Christianity and Professional Social Work." DSW dissertation, University of Pennsylvania.

Ellis, Albert. 1980. "Psychotherapy and Atheistic Values." *Journal of Consulting and Clinical Psychology* 48:635–39.

Faver, Catherine A. 1985. "Religious Beliefs, Professional Values, and Social Work." Paper presented at Council on Social Work Education Annual Program Meeting, Washington, D.C., February 1985.

Festinger, Leon. 1957. *A Theory of Cognitive Dissonance.* New York: Harper and Row.

Filsinger, Erik E. and Margarit R. Wilson. 1984. "Religiosity, Socioeconomic Rewards and Family Development: Predictors of Marital Adjustment." *Journal of Marriage and Family* 46:663–70.

Fishkin, James S. 1982. *The Limits of Obligation.* New Haven: Yale University Press.

Flax, James W. et al. 1979. *Mental Health in Rural America.* Washington, D.C.: National Institute of Mental Health.

Frank, Jerome. 1972. *The Revolution of Hope: Toward a Humanized Technology.* New York: Bantam Books.

—— 1978. "The Medical Power of Faith." *Human Nature* 1(8):40–47.

Frankl, Victor. 1963. *Man's Search for Meaning.* New York: Pocketbooks.

—— 1968(1957). *The Doctor and the Soul.* New York: Knopf.

Freud, Sigmund. 1946. *Civilization and Its Discontent.* J. Riviere, tr. London: Hogarth Press.

—— 1928. *The Future of an Illusion.* W. D. Robson-Scott, tr. London: Horace Liveright.

Frey, Jackie L. 1973. "Social Work Students' Opinions Regarding Religious Issues in Case Work Practice." Unpublished MSW thesis, Smith College School of Social Work, Northampton, Mass.

Galanter, Marc. 1980. "Psychological Induction into the Large-Group: Findings from a Modern Religious Sect." *American Journal of Psychiatry* 137:1574–79.

—— 1982. "Charismatic Religious Sects and Psychiatry: An Overview." *American Journal of Psychiatry* 139:1539–48.

Galanter, Marc and Peter Buckley. 1978. "Evangelical Religion and Meditation: Psychotherapeutic Effects." *Journal of Nervous and Mental Diseases* 166:685–91.

Gallup, George, Jr. 1980. *Religion in America 1979–80.* Princeton: Princeton Religion Research Center.

—— 1985. "Religion in America: 50 Years." *The Gallup Report* No. 236.

—— 1986. *The Gallup Report* No. 244–45.

Gass, Carlton S. 1984. "Orthodox Christian Values Related to Psychotherapy and Mental Health." *Journal of Psychology and Theology* 12:230–37.

Gatza, M. 1979. "The Role of Healing Prayer in the Helping Process." *Social Thought* 5(2):3–13.

Gilbert, Alan D. 1980. *The Making of Post-Christian Britain*. London: Longman.

Ginsburg, S. W. 1950. "Values and the Psychiatrist." *American Journal of Orthopsychiatry* 20:466–78.

Glasser, Paul H. 1984. "Being Honest with Ourselves: What Happens When Our Values Conflict with Our Clients'?" *Practice Digest* 6(4):6–10.

Glick, Peter M. 1977. "Individualism, Society, and Social Work." *Social Casework* 58:579–84.

Glock, Charles Y. and Robert Stark. 1965. *Religion and Society in Tension*. Chicago: Rand McNally.

Goldstein, Howard. 1986. "The Neglected Moral Link in Social Work Practice." *Social Work* 31:352–57.

Gollub, S. L. 1974. "A Critical Look at Religious Requirements in Adoption." *Public Welfare* 32(2):23–28.

Goode, William Jr. 1969. "The Theoretical Limits of Professionalization." In A. Etzioni, ed., *The Semi-Professions and Their Organization*, pp. 266–313. New York: Free Press.

Gordon, David F. 1984. "Dying to Self: Self-Control Through Abandonment." *Sociological Analysis* 45:41–56.

Gordon, William E. 1965a. "Knowledge and Value: Their Distinction and Relationship in Clarifying Social Work Practice." *Social Work* 10(3):32–39.

—— 1965b. "Toward a Social Work Frame of Reference." *Journal for Education in Social Work* 1:19–26.

Gouldner, Alvin W. 1973. *For Sociology: Renewal and Critique in Sociology Today*. New York: Basic Books.

Greeley, Andrew M. 1981. *The Religious Imagination*. Los Angeles: Sadlier.

Gunsalus, Catherine L. 1969. "The Impact of Social Revolutions on Values." In *The Social Welfare Forum 1969*, pp. 130–41. New York: Columbia University Press.

Gurin, Gerald, Joseph Veroff, and Sheila Feld. 1960. *Americans View Their Mental Health*. New York: Basic Books.

Guy, Mary E. 1985. *Professionals in Organizations*. New York: Praeger.

Guzzetta, Charles. 1966. "Concepts and Precepts in Social Work Education." *Journal for Education in Social Work* 2(2):40–47.

Habermas, J. 1971. *Toward a Rational Society*. J. Shapiro, tr. Boston: Beacon Press.

Halevy, H. D. 1983. *Mekor Hayim*. Tel Aviv: Author (Hebrew).

Hall, M. Penelope and Ismene V. Howes. 1965. *The Church in Social Work*. London: Routledge and Kegan Paul.

Hammond, Phillip E. and Benton Johnson, eds. 1970. *American Mosaic: Social Patterns of Religion in the United States*. New York: Random House.

Handler, Joel F. and Ellen Jane Hollingsworth. 1971. *The Deserving Poor.* Chicago: Markham.

Hansen, Marcus Lee. 1952. "The Third Generation in America." *Commentary* (November), 14: 492–500.

Hardiker, Pauline and Mary Barker, eds. 1981. *Theories of Practice in Social Work.* London: Academic Press.

Heisenberg, Werner. 1958. *Physics and Philosophy: The Revolution in Modern Science.* New York: Harper.

Henry, W. E., J. H. Sims, and S. L. Spray. 1971. *The Fifth Profession: Becoming a Psychotherapist.* San Francisco: Jossey-Bass.

Herskovitz, Melville. 1947. *Man and His Works.* New York: Knopf.

Higgins, P. C. and G. L. Albrecht. 1977. "Hellfire and Delinquency Revisited." *Social Forces* 55:952–58.

Hirschi, T. and R. Stark. 1969. "Hellfire and Delinquency." *Social Problems* 17:202–13.

Hoge, Dean R. and Ernesto DeZulueta. 1985. "Salience as a Condition for Various Consequences of Religious Commitment." *Journal for the Scientific Study of Religion* 24(1):21–38.

Howard, Donald S. 1969. *Social Welfare: Values, Means, and Ends.* New York: Random House.

Howell-Thomas, Dorothy. 1974. *Mutual Understanding: The Social Services and Christian Belief.* London: Church Information Office.

Humphries, Robert H. 1982. "Therapeutic Neutrality Reconsidered." *Journal of Religion and Health* 21:124–31.

Huntington, James. 1893. "Philanthropy and Morality." *Philanthropy and Social Progress.* Jane Addams, ed. New York: Crowell.

Hurley, James B. 1981. *Men and Women in Biblical Perspective.* Grand Rapids, Mich.: Zondervan.

Imre, Roberta E. 1971. "A Theological View of Social Casework." *Social Casework* 52:578–85.

Jacquent, Constant H. Jr., ed. 1983. *Yearbook of American and Canadian Churches.* Nashville, Tenn.: Abingdon Press.

James, William. 1936(1902). *Varieties of Religious Experience.* New York: Modern Library.

Jameson, J. Franklin. 1967(1925). *The American Revolution Reconsidered as a Social Movement.* Princeton: Princeton University Press.

Johnson, Benton. 1961. "Do Holy Sects Socialize in Dominant Values?" *Social Forces* 39:309–16.

——1957. "A Critical Appraisal of the Church-Sect Typology." *American Sociological Review* 22:88–92.

Johnson, F. Ernest. 1941. "Protestant Social Work." In R. H. Kurtz, ed., *Social Work Year Book,* pp. 403–12. New York: Russell Sage Foundation,

Jones, Howard, ed. 1975. *Towards a New Social Work.* London: Routledge and Kegan Paul.

Jones, N. D. et al. 1985. "Using the Religious Community as Family in Psychiatric Treatment." *Bulletin of the Menninger Clinic* 49(5):466–74.

Jordon, William K. 1959. *Philanthropy in England 1480–1660*. New York: Russell Sage Foundation.

Joseph, M. Vincentia and Ann Patrick. 1980. "A Parish Neighborhood Model of Social Work Practice." *Social Casework* 61:423–32.

Judah, Eleanor Hannon. 1985. "A Sprituality of Professional Service: A Sacramental Model." *Social Thought* 11(4):25–35.

Jung, C. G. 1961. *Memories, Dreams, Reflections*. New York: Pantheon Books.

Kadushin, Alfred. 1972. *The Social Work Interview*. New York: Columbia University Press.

Kadushin, Alfred and C. F. Wieringa. 1960. "A Comparison: Dutch and American Expectations Regarding Behavior of the Caseworker." *Social Casework* 41:503–11.

Kahn, Jack and Elspeth Earle. 1982. *The Cry for Help and the Professional Response*. Oxford: Pergamon Press.

Kane, Rosalie A. 1986. "High Technology and Psychosocial Well-Being." Barbara Berkman, ed. *Social Work in Health Care Lectures*, pp. 12–25. Boston: Massachusetts General Hospital Institute of Health Professions.

Kaslow, Florence and Marvin B. Sussman, eds. 1982. *Cults and the Family*. New York: Haworth.

Keefe, Thomas. 1976. "Empathy: The Critical Skill." *Social Work* 21:10–14.

Keith-Lucas, Alan. 1960. "Some Notes on Theology and Social Work." *Social Casework* 41:87–91.

—— 1971. "Ethics in Social Work." *Encyclopedia of Social Work*. R. Morris et al., eds. New York: National Association of Social Workers, pp. 324–28.

—— 1972. *Giving and Taking Help*. Chapel Hill: University of North Carolina Press.

King, Morton. 1967. "Measuring the Religious Variable: Nine Proposed Dimensions." *Journal for the Scientific Study of Religion* 6:173–90.

Kluckhohn, Clyde et al. 1951. "Values and Value-Orientations in the Theory of Action." In T. Parsons and E. A, Shils, eds. *Toward a General Theory of Action*, pp. 388–433, Cambridge: Harvard University Press.

Kossal, S. and R. Kane. 1980. "Self-Determination Dissected." *Clinical Social Work Journal* 8:161–78.

Kuhn, Thomas S. 1970. *The Structure of Scientific Revolutions*. 2d ed. Chicago: University of Chicago Press.

Kung, Hans. 1979. *Freud and the Problem of God*. New Haven: Yale University Press.

Landers, Ann. 1986. "Memories of Being Pregnant at Sixteen." *Boston Globe*, December 31, 1986, p. 31.

Lee, Dorothy. 1953. "Are Basic Needs Ultimate?" In C. Kluckhohn and A. H. Murray, eds., *Personality in Nature, Society and Culture*, pp. 335–41. 2d rev. ed. New York: Knopf.

Lenin, V. I. 1940(1905). "Socialism and Religion." *Religion*, pp. 11–15. London: Lawrence and Wishart.

Lenski, Gerhard. 1961. *The Religious Factor*. Garden City, N.Y.: Doubleday.

Lerner, Daniel and Harold Lasswell, eds. 1951. *The Policy Science.* Stanford: Stanford University Press.

Levine, Edward M. 1980. "Deprogramming Without Tears." *Society* 17:34–42.

Levy, Charles. 1976a. "Personal Versus Professional Values: The Practitioner's Dilemma." *Clinical Social Work Journal* 4:110–20.

—— 1976b. *Social Work Ethics.* New York: Human Science Press.

Light, Donald, Jr. 1979. "Uncertainty and Control in Professional Training." *Journal of Health and Social Behavior* 20:310–22.

Loewenberg, Frank M. 1983. *Fundamentals of Social Intervention.* 2d ed. New York: Columbia University Press.

Loewenberg, Frank M. and Ralph Dolgoff. 1985. *Ethical Decisions for Social Work Practice.* 2d ed. Itasca, Ill.: Peacock.

London, P. 1976. "Psychopathology for Religious Neurosis." *Journal of Consulting and Clinical Psychology* 44:145–46.

Luckman, Thomas. 1967. *The Invisible Religion.* New York: Macmillan.

Luther, Martin. 1931. *The Bondage of Will.* H. Cole, tr. Grand Rapids, Mich.: Eerdmans.

Macarov, David. 1978. "Empathy: The Charismatic Chimera." *Journal of Education for Social Work* 14(3): 86–92.

McCarthy, Kathleen D. 1982. *Noblesse Oblige: Charity and Cultural Philanthropy in Chicago 1849–1929.* Chicago: University of Chicago Press.

McCormick, Mary J. 1975. *Enduring Values in a Changing Society.* New York: Family Service Association of America.

McLemore, C. W. and J. H. Court. 1977. "Religion and Psychotherapy: Ethics, Civil Liberties and Clinical Savvy." *Journal of Consulting and Clinical Psychology* 45:1172–75.

McLeod, Donna L. and Henry J. Meyer. 1967. "A Study of the Values of Social Workers." In E. Thomas, ed., *Behavioral Science for Social Workers,* pp. 401–16. New York: Free Press.

McMinn, Mark R. 1984. "Religious Values and Client-Therapist Matching in Psychotherapy." *Journal of Psychology and Theology* 12 (Spring): 24–33.

Maimonides, Moses. 1956. *Guide for the Perplexed.* M. Friedlander tr., New York: Dover.

Malony, H. Newton and A. Adams Lovekin. 1985. *Glossolalia: Behavioral Science Perspectives on Speaking in Tongues.* New York: Oxford University Press.

Maluccio, Anthony N. 1979. *Learning from Clients.* New York: Free Press.

Manese, Joanne E. and William E. Sedlacek. 1983. *Changes in Religious Behavior and Attitudes of College Students by Race and Sex Over a Ten-Year Period.* College Park: University of Maryland Counseling Center.

Marty, Martin E. 1980. "Social Service: Godly and Godless." *Social Service Review* 54:463–81.

Marx, Karl 1963. "Contribution to the Critique of Hegel's Philosophy of Right." *Early Writings.* T.B. Bottomore, tr. London: C.A. Watts.

Maslow, Abraham H. 1962. *The Further Reaches of Human Nature.* New York: Penguin Books.

—— 1969. "Toward a Humanistic Biology." *American Psychologist* 24:724–35.

—— 1970(1964). *Religion, Values and Peak-Experiences.* New York: Viking.

Mather, Cotton. 1966(1710). *Bonifacius: An Essay Upon the Good.* D. Levin, ed. Cambridge: Harvard University Press.

Menninger, Karl. 1973. *Whatever Became of Sin?* New York: Hawthorne Books.

Meyer, Jacob C. 1930. *Church and State in Massachusetts: 1740–1833.* Cleveland, Ohio: Western Reserve University Press.

Meystedt, Diana M. 1984. "Religion and the Rural Population: Implications for Social Work." *Social Casework* 65:219–26.

Michels, Robert. 1959. *Political Parties.* E. and C. Paul, trs. New York: Dover.

Mitchell, K. M., J. D. Bozarth, and C. C. Krauft. 1977. "A Reappraisal of the Therapeutic Effectiveness of Accurate Empathy, Nonpossessive Warmth, and Genuineness." In A. S. Gurman and A. M. Razin, eds., *Effective Psychotherapy: A Handbook of Research,* pp. 482–502. New York: Pergamon Press.

Moberg, David O. 1982. "The Salience of Religion in Everyday Life: Selected Evidence from Survey Research in Sweden and America." *Sociological Analysis* 43:205–17.

Mobley, W. H. and E. A. Locke. 1970. "The Relationship of Value Importance and Satisfaction." *Organizational Behavior and Human Performance* 5:463–83.

More, Thomas. 1922(1516). *Utopia.* Cambridge: Cambridge University Press.

Morland, John. 1958. *Millways of Kent.* Chapel Hill: University of North Carolina Press.

Mullen, E. J. 1969. "Differences in Worker Styles in Casework." *Social Casework* 50:347–53.

National Association of Social Workers (NASW). 1978. *Compilations of Public Policy Statements.* New York: NASW.

—— 1980. *Code of Ethics of the NASW.* Silver Springs, Md.: NASW.

—— 1985. *NASW Data Bank: Selected Tables.* Silver Springs, Md.: NASW.

National Center for Health Statistics. C. A. Bachrach and M. C. Horn. 1985. "Marriage and First Intercourse . . . 1982." *Advance Data from Vital and Health Statistics* No. 107. Hyatsville, Md.: U.S. Public Health Service.

National Conference of Catholic Charities (NCCC). 1983a. *A Code of Ethics.* Washington, D.C.: NCCC.

——1983b. *1982 Annual Survey.* Washington, D.C.: NCCC.

Ness, R. C. and R. M. Wintrob. 1980. "The Emotional Impact of Fundamentalist Religious Participation: An Empirical Study of Intergroup Variation." *American Journal of Orthopsychiatry* 50:302–15.

Netting, F. Ellen. 1984. "Church-Related Agencies and Social Welfare." *Social Service Review* 58:404–20.

Neuhaus, Richard J. 1985. "What the Fundamentalists Want." *Commentary* 79(5):41–46.

Nichols, Abigail C. 1979. "Social Workers and/or Philosophers: Value Content in the Social Welfare Policy and Services Curriculum." Paper presented at Annual Program Meeting, Council on Social Work Education, Boston.

Niebuhr, H. Richard. 1929. *The Social Sources of Denominationalism.* New York: Holt.

—— 1937. *The Kingdom of God in America.* New York: Harper.

Niebuhr, Reinhold. 1932. *The Contribution of Religion to Social Work.* New York: Columbia University Press.

—— 1958. *Pious and Secular America.* New York: Scribner's.

Nilsen, E. Anker. 1980. *Religion and Personality Integration.* Uppsala, Sweden: Acta Universitatis Upsaliensis.

O'Leary, K. P. and G. T. Wilson. 1975. *Behavior Therapy: Application and Outcome.* Englewood Cliffs, N. J.: Prentice-Hall.

Olmstead, Clifton E. 1970. "Social Religion in Urban America." In P. E. Hammond and B. Johnson, eds., *American Mosaic,* pp. 139–48. New York: Random House.

Parsons, Talcott. 1951. *The Social System.* Glencoe, Ill.: Free Press.

—— 1961. "Religion and Social Structure." In T. Parsons et al., eds., *Theories of Society,* 1: 645–46. New York: Free Press.

Pattison, E. Mansell. 1980. "Religious Youth Cults: Alternative Healing Social Networks." *Journal of Religion and Health* 19:275–86.

Perlman, Helen H. 1976. "Believing and Doing: Values in Social Work Education." *Social Casework* 57:381–90.

Peteet, J. R. 1981. "Issues in the Treatment of Religious Patients." *American Journal of Psychotherapy* 35:559–64.

Philp, Mark. 1979. "Notes on the Form of Knowledge in Social Work." *Sociological Review* 27:83–111.

Pilseker, Carlton. 1978. "Values: A Problem for Everyone." *Social Work* 23:54–57.

Pins, Arnulf M. 1960. "What Specific Content on Religion Should Be Included and Where Should It Come?" *Religious Content in Social Work Education,* pp. 56–70. Annual Program Meeting, Council on Social Work Education. Mimeograph.

Poblete, Renato and Thomas O'Dea. 1960. "Anomie and the 'Quest for Community': The Formation of Sects Among the Puerto Ricans of New York." *American Catholic Sociological Review* 21(1):25–35.

Pope, Liston. 1942. *Millhands and Preachers.* New Haven: Yale University Press.

Potts, Leah. 1971. "Counseling Women with Unwanted Pregnancies." In F. Hazelkorn, ed., *Family Planning.* New York: Council on Social Work Education.

Pullan, B. 1971 *Rich and Poor in Renaissance Venice.* London: Blackwell.

—— 1976. "Catholics and the Poor in Early Modern Europe." *Transactions of the Royal Historical Society,* 26: 15–34. 5th series, London.

Pumphrey, Muriel W. 1959. *The Teaching of Values and Ethics in Social Work Education.* Council on Social Work Education (CSWE) Curriculum Study vol. 13. New York: CSWE.

Quebedeaux, Richard. 1974. *The Young Evangelicals: Revolution in Orthodoxy.* New York: Harper and Row.

Rayburn, Carole A. 1985. "The Religious Patient's Initial Encounter with Psychotherapy." In E. M. Stern, ed., *Psychotherapy and the Religiously Committed Patient*, pp. 35–45. New York: Haworth Press.

Reamer, Frederic G. 1983. "The Free Will–Determinism Debate and Social Work." *Social Service Review* 57:626–44.

Rees, S. 1978. *Social Work Face to Face*. London: Arnold.

Reid, William. 1977. "Sectarian Agencies." *Encyclopedia of Social Work*. 17th issue, Washington, D.C.: National Association of Social Workers, 2:1244–54.

Reid, William and Patricia Hanrahan. 1982. "Recent Evaluations of Social Work: Grounds for Optimism." *Social Work* 27:328–40.

Reid, William and Peter K. Stimpson. 1987. "Sectarian Agencies." *Encyclopedia of Social Work*. 18th ed. Silver Springs, Md.: National Association of Social Workers, 2: 545–56.

Richmond, Mary. 1917. *Social Diagnosis*. New York: Russell Sage Foundation.

Rockowitz, R. J., J. W. Korpela, and K. C. Hunter. 1981. "Social Work Dilemma: When Religion and Medicine Clash." *Health and Social Work* 6(4):5–11.

Rosen, Aaron and R. S. Connaway. 1969. "Public Welfare, Social Work and Social Work Education." *Social Work* 14:87–94.

Rumberger, D. J. and M. L. Rogers. 1982. "Pastoral Openness to Interaction with a Private Christian Counseling Service." *Journal of Psychology and Theology* 10:337–45.

Rutman, Darretts B. 1965. *Winthrop's Boston: Portrait of a Puritan Town, 1630–1649*. Chapel Hill: University of North Carolina Press.

Salomon, E. L. 1967. "Humanistic Values and Social Casework." *Social Casework* 48:26–32.

Sanford, John A. 1977. *Healing and Wholeness*. New York: Paulist Press.

Scanoni, L. and V. Mollenkott. 1978. *Is the Homosexual My Neighbor? Another Christian View*. New York: Harper and Row.

Schroeder, W. Widick et al. 1974. *Suburban Religion*. Chicago: Center for the Scientific Study of Religion.

Shils, Edward. 1968. "Ritual and Crisis." In D. R. Cutler, ed. *The Religious Situation: 1968*. Boston: Beacon Press.

Siporin, Max. 1975. *Introduction to Social Work Practice*. New York: Macmillan.

—— 1984. "A Future for Social Work Education." In M. Dinerman and L. L. Geismar, eds., *A Quarter-Century of Social Work Education*, pp. 237–51. Washington, D.C.: National Association of Social Workers/Council an Social Work Education

—— 1985a. "Deviance, Morality and Social Work Therapy." *Social Thought* 11(4):11–24.

—— 1985b. "Current Social Work Perspectives for Clinical Practice." *Clinical Social Work Journal* 13:198–217.

Siporin, Max and Paul Glasser. 1987. "Family Functioning, Morality, and Therapy." P. Glasser and D. Watkins, eds. *Religion and Social Work*. Beverly Hills: Sage.

Skinner, B. F. 1964. "Behaviorism at Fifty." In T. W. Wann, ed., *Behaviorism and Phenomenology* pp. 79–97. Chicago: University of Chicago Press.

Slater, Philip. 1970. *The Pursuit of Loneliness*. Boston: Beacon Press.

Smith, Timothy L. 1957. *Revivalism and Social Reform in Mid-Nineteenth Century America*. New York: Abingdon Press.

Sneck, William J. and Ronald P. Bonica. 1980. "Attempting the Integration of Psychology and Spirituality." *Social Thought* 6(3):27–36.

Soloveitchik, J. B. 1986. *The Halakhic Mind: An Essay on Jewish Tradition and Modern Thought*. New York: Seth Press.

Sombart, Werner. 1915. *The Quintessence of Capitalism*. M. Epstein, tr. New York: Dutton.

Sorrentino, Mary Ann. 1986. "My Church Threw Me Out." *Redbook* (June), 167:14–20.

Spencer, Sue. 1956. "Religion and Social Work." *Social Work* 1(3):19–26.

Spero, Moshe Halevi, ed. 1980. *Judaism and Psychology: Halachic Perspectives*. New York: Ktav.

—— 1985. *Psychotherapy of the Religious Patient*. Springfield, Ill.: Thomas.

Spinoza, Baruch. 1955. *Ethics*. J. Guttman, ed. New York: Modern Library.

Star, Barbara. 1980. "Patterns in Family Violence." *Social Casework* 61:339–46.

Stark, R. 1971. "Psychopathology and Religious Commitment." *Review of Religious Research* 12:165–75.

Stark, Rodney and Charles Glock. 1970. *American Piety: The Nature of Religious Commitment*. Berkeley: University of California Press.

Stern, E. Mark, ed. 1985. *Psychotherapy and the Religiously Committed Patient*. New York: Haworth Press.

Stones, Christopher R. 1978. "The Jesus People: Fundamentalism and Changes Associated with Consent." *Journal for the Scientific Study of Religion* 17:155–58.

Stovich, Raymond J. 1985. "Metaphor and Therapy: Theory, Technique and Practice of the Use of Religious Imagery in Therapy." In E. M. Stern, ed., *Psychotheraphy and the Religiously Committed Patient*, pp. 117–22. New York: Haworth Press.

Sweet, William Warren. 1944. *Revivalism in America*. New York: Scribner's.

Swissair. 1985. *Public Holidays Around the World 1986*. Zurich.

Thomas, Lewis. 1981. "The Scientific Method and the Puzzles of Nature." *The Atlantic Monthly*. Reprinted in *Dialogue*, no. 56, pp. 65–68.

Thomlison, Ray J. 1984. "Something Works: Evidence from Practice Effectiveness Studies." *Social Work* 29:51–56.

Tierney, Brian. 1959. *Medieval Poor Law*. Berkeley: University of California Press.

Timms, Noel. 1983. *Social Work Values: An Enquiry*. London: Routledge and Kegan Paul.

Titmuss, Richard M. 1974. *Social Policy*. London: Allen and Unwin.

Todd, A. 1920. *The Scientific Spirit of Social Work*. New York: Macmillan.

Tomko, Barbara. 1985. "Creating Access to Rituals." *Social Work* 30:72–73.

Towle, Charlotte. 1965(1945). *Common Human Needs*. New York: National Association of Social Workers.

Troeltsch, Ernst. 1931(1912). *The Social Teachings of the Christian Churches*. O. Wyon, tr. New York: Macmillan.

Tyrrell, Bernard J. 1982. *Christotherapy II*. New York: Paulist Press.

Underwood, Kenneth. 1957. *Protestants and Catholics*. Boston: Beacon Press.

Vigilante, Joseph. 1974. "Between Values and Science: Education for the Profession During a Moral Crisis or Is Proof Truth." *Journal of Education for Social Work* 10:107–15.

Walch, Timothy. 1978. "Catholic Social Institutions and Urban Development." *Catholic Historical Review* 64:16–32.

Walls, Gary B. 1980. "Values and Psychotherapy: A Comment." *Journal of Consulting and Clinical Psychology* 48:640–41.

Weber, Max. 1958(1904–5). *The Protestant Ethic and the Spirit of Capitalism*. T. Parsons, tr. New York: Scribner's.

—— 1963. *The Sociology of Religion*. E. Fischoff, tr. Boston: Beacon Press.

Weiss, J. O. 1982. "Religion and Genetics: The Possible Effect of Good Pastoral Care on Genetic Counseling Clinics." *Social Thought* 8(2):2–7.

White, R. H. 1970. "Toward a Theory of Religious Influence." In P. E. Hammond and B. Johnson, eds. *American Mosaic*, pp. 14–23. New York: Random House.

Whitehead, Alfred N. 1948. *Science and the New World*. New York: Macmillan.

Will, George. 1980. "The Ringing Grooves of Change." *Boston Globe*, May 26, p. 18.

Williams, Robin M. Jr. 1967. "Individual and Group Values." *The Annals* 371:20–37.

Wilson, Bryan R. 1982. *Religion in Sociological Perspective*. New York: Oxford University Press.

Wimberley, Dale W. 1984. "Socioeconomic Deprivation and Religious Salience: A Cognitive Behavioral Approach." *Sociological Quarterly* 25:229–38.

Worthington, Everett L., Jr. and Gary C. Scott. 1983. "Goal Selection for Counseling with Potentially Religious Clients. . . . " *Journal of Psychology and Theology* 11(4):318–29.

Wuthnow, Robert, ed. 1979. *The Religious Dimension: New Directions*. New York: Academic Press.

Yankelovich, Daniel. 1974. *The New Morality*. New York: McGraw-Hill.

—— 1981. *New Rules*. New York: Random House.

Yelloly, Margaret. 1980. *Social Work Theory and Psychoanalysis*. London: Van Nostrand Reinhold.

Yinger, John M. 1957. *Religion, Society, and the Individual*. New York: Macmillan.

—— 1970. *The Scientific Study of Religion*. New York: Macmillan.

Zilboorg, G. 1962. *Psychoanalysis and Religion*. London: Farrar Strauss Giroux.

Name Index

Subject Index